# Don't Go

## The Mystery of I

## by Svetlana Oss

# Contents

# Introduction

In Mikailovskoe cemetery in the Russian city of Yekaterinburg, on the eastern edge of the Ural Mountains, there is a monument to nine students who died while on an expedition to the sub-polar Urals in the winter of 1959.

Even today, nobody knows exactly how they lost their lives.

The official government investigation states enigmatically that the students perished as the result of an 'overwhelming force,' but no one knows what this force was, or where it came from.

I've never been a fan of horror stories. This one, though, is a very peculiar kind of horror story, and in my view an exceptionally interesting one. For one thing, it's a true story, and extremely well documented; it also has many puzzling quirks and contradictions. Above all, at the core of the story there is a seemingly unfathomable mystery.

Most apparently logical theories on what happened to the students, falter when exposed to the evidence, and there is usually at least one fact that completely contradicts whatever theory one prefers. This excites people. It certainly excites me.

I first became interested in the story, which is known as the Dyatlov Pass tragedy, in February 2008. I had heard about it when I was a girl of about 14, but that was in the early 1980s, during the days of the Soviet Union, and it was a very vague story. The suppression of information in Russia at that time ensured that the incident and its aftermath were kept as quiet as possible by the Soviet government, which found it embarrassing that nine students had died in the most mysterious of circumstances on a snowy, wind-beaten mountainside.

Wasn't the Soviet government supposed to have all the answers? It certainly didn't have the answer to this particular mystery, so it was hardly surprising that the government wanted to hush things up. But then came Mikhail Gorbachev, *glasnost* and *perestroika*, and gradually more details about the Dyatlov Pass tragedy began to emerge.

In 2008, when I was working as a journalist, I came across some basic information about the tragedy, and I remembered hearing about it when I was a girl. Now, I plunged into the research in earnest. A few weeks later, I published an article about the event in *The Moscow Times*, an English-language Russian newspaper. As far as I am aware, this was the first-ever article written in English about the event.

I was amazed at the attention the article received. I had calls from Hollywood screenwriters, and I saw my research material used in other people's articles and blogs around the world.

Certainly, I can't help being proud that my original article has played some role in bringing the Dyatlov Pass tragedy to the attention of the world beyond Russia. Today, Dyatlov Pass tragedy is world-famous.

Since then, there have been books, TV documentaries and even a movie (a fairly weird movie, to be honest) about the Dyatlov Pass tragedy. I wanted to write a book of my own, but I knew that I could do so only when I had, as far as I could know, marshalled all the facts.

As part of my research, I went to Yekaterinburg and spoke to people who had been involved in the original investigation. I also had the privilege of talking to Yuri Yudin, the tenth member of the Dyatlov group. Yuri owed his survival to his early departure from the expedition due to his sciatica.

Eventually, in 2013, I began to write this book. I wrote it in English, because I wanted it to be read by people beyond Russia's borders.

I believe I have found the answer to the Dyatlov Pass mystery. I present it in this book, which I dedicate to all the members of the Dyatlov group who were denied the lives they should have had. Throughout all my research, I have never forgotten that the bodies that were brought down from the mountain were once admirable young people, full of life.

They did not deserve to die so young, and especially not in the way they did. But it happened, and their story deserves to be told.

# PART I: THE ADVENTURE

# 1

Two middle-aged men are quietly talking together across a wide and highly-polished wooden desk. Across the marbled reception lobby outside the open office door, a clock ticks. This is the only sound in an area flanked by oil paintings and hovering plainclothes security men. In the manner of old soldiers who are asked the intrusive question 'how was your war?', the conversation of the two men is conditioned by their memories of the hardships and danger they suffered, under unrelenting authority, when they were in the army. They speak in an amicable way, but they are not friends; they are merely men of similar education, similar intellect and from similar backgrounds. They can look each other in the eyes with a mutual respect, despite their different stations and status.

The stouter of the two men is Boris Yeltsin, at that time the First Secretary of the Sverdlovsk Communist Party. The lean, rangy one is Vladimir Korotaev, senior litigator and legal adviser to the Regional Prosecutor's Office in Sverdlovsk, now Yekaterinburg.

Yeltsin had been a student at the prestigious Ural Polytechnic Institute, the top Russian university, in Yekaterinburg. In 1976, when he became the First Secretary of the Communist Party in Sverdlovsk, one of the first things he did was to invite Vladimir Korotaev, the first investigator of the Dyatlov case, to a private meeting.

The men exchange a few pleasantries before Yeltsin leans forward and, in a low and friendly voice, broaches the subject he wants to discuss. 'I'm extremely interested, Vladimir Ivanovich,' says Yeltsin, using the familiar Russian patronymic, 'in exactly how these students could have died in the way they did. I myself am a former student of the Ural Polytechnic Institute, like the climbers who went on the trip. I heard *what* happened, but I could never understand *how* it happened.'

Boris Yeltsin's lifelong fascination is shared by almost everyone who has heard of the Dyatlov Pass tragedy: the events were so devastating, so unusual, so deeply investigated and yet so resistant to understanding. Many Russians remember the breaking news, and the civic outrage that it stirred, as a life event. By the time of this meeting in the Kremlin,    the mystery had been   unsolved for thirty years.

Korotaev recalls how his local Communist Party leader, Ivan Prodanov, had banned him from continuing the investigation after only a few days. Prodanov had told him that: 'this case is being investigated under the gaze of Khrushchev, and I have assured him that it was just hypothermia. These people just froze to death.'

Korotaev also recalls the events on Mount 1079, where the members of the Dyatlov group died. He remembers how he had flown in by helicopter to that bleak slope: he remembers how small, how abandoned, and how smashed the tent had looked; it was as if someone had taken a child's shelter into one of the most inhospitable places in the world, a place of ferocious winds and heavy snow, often prey to blizzards and severe storms, a place regarded as sacred by the local people, the Mansi. It made him think of the courageous and determined fight for survival that they had discovered, by young people at the end of their strength in a place where no one could survive. He had known he could not agree to the betrayal of that superhuman effort.

'I'm afraid I don't believe that the deaths of the students were simply caused by hypothermia, Comrade Prodanov,' Korotaev had said.

Korotaev said much the same thing to Yeltsin that day when they met.

'Boris Nikolayevich, I'll tell you openly about it. I think it was murder, and not a 'normal" murder - but what they wrote when they closed the criminal case was true. They were killed by *an overwhelming force*.'

Yeltsin snorted.

'Yes, there is such an overwhelming force, and maybe we both can guess what it is,' he said. 'Tomorrow I'll call the Central Committee of the Communist Party and ask them to reopen the criminal case.' Yeltsin knew the country he lived in. He clearly suspected a cover-up.

Korotaev could not help feeling relieved. Would the truth now, at last, come out?

He and Yeltsin shook hands and parted.

Many years have passed since that conversation took place, but the criminal case was never reopened; not even Boris Yeltsin's influence and power was able to achieve that. An 'overwhelming force' had killed the victims on the mountain. Another overwhelming force was conspiring to keep what had happened on the mountain a secret.

# 2

*'It's the last day of preparations and everything has been quite hectic. From eleven in the morning I was scampering between stores buying different bits and pieces. And I was silly enough to buy five metres of cambric which cost 200 roubles. I was packing in such a rush and of course I've forgotten one of my sweaters! Everyone was busy with something, and we had so many things to arrange!'*

(From Lyuda Dubinina's personal diary January 23, 1959)

Lyuda Dubinina

The snowy January of 1959 was eventful for Lyuda Dubinina, a 20-year-old who studied engineering and economics at the Ural Polytechnic Institute (UPI) in Sverdlovsk. For one thing, her dream had finally come true: she was going on a mountain expedition as a member of the city's best hiking team. She was the one who suggested the whole adventure. She was the one who endeavoured to make it happen. Just a week before the expedition set off, Lyuda's family had moved from their communal flat on Mamin Sibiryak Street to a private, two-room apartment in the centre of Sverdlovsk.

The Dubinin family had been living in a cramped communal apartment. The shortage of living space after the Russian Revolution led to routine sharing of kitchen and toilet facilities by families. This often created the special psychological conditions that led to mass spying and informing on each other. Every apartment seemed to house a madman, a drunk, a troublemaker and a snitch. They all had to live within a power hierarchy and to follow rules governing everyday behaviour: the so-called Rules of Procedure. And finally it had happened: the Dubinins had moved somewhere nicer. So, no more quarrels in the kitchen, no more annoying and unpleasant remarks from the neighbours such as *You should turn the toilet light off after you, or I will apply for your eviction.'*

In the new apartment, Lyuda's younger brother, Vladimir, was running about the empty rooms exclaiming: *'Hurray! Freedom!'*

A friend of Lyuda's, Galina Batalova, recalls how happy Lyuda was during these days. Her parents wanted her to spend the school holidays at home but the girl was determined to participate in the mountain expedition. 'She was so excited to be accepted into the group... She looked kind of spiritual, - she wanted to be fit and did lots of ski training.'

Lyuda had already been on several expeditions; once she had even lead a group on a medium-difficulty route in the northern Urals. There was a rather unusual combination of shyness and strength in her: a city girl and the daughter of a senior manager, she could easily blush when talking to boys but did not shed a tear when a hunter's stray bullet struck her leg.

When it comes to heading to the mountains to brave the elements, and perhaps to find oneself, it's all about making sure you're going with the right people. It was hard for Lyuda to organize the group by herself. It was no easy task for a young woman to lead a group of men into the mountains, but Lyuda had no problem dealing with the opposite sex, in spite of the attitudes she frequently encountered. In her diary she writes of Eugene Zinoviev, a fellow student: 'Yevgeny is constantly trying to put me down. He must take me for some stupid girl.'

Rustem Slobodin

Lyuda knew she could rely on Rustem Slobodin, who had been in her group a year ago. Aside from being heavily involved in sports, this grey-eyed fellow with prominent cheek bones and open countenance was very dependable. Ethnically, he was Russian but his parents, both university professors, worked in Asia when he was born and gave him an Asian name. Rustem, or Rustik as he was often called, was a man of few words, who would share with you his last piece of bread – not a trivial thing when food stores were basic and the Explorer's Club stores were often low.

Courageous and hardened, Rustem had one rather sentimental passion: he played the mandolin and always took this extravagant piece of luggage with him on expeditions. It looked strange in his big, rough arms when he played it at night, sitting by the fire.

Another person who readily agreed to go with Lyuda was Yuri Yudin, a kind-hearted guy who was always smiling and who felt almost like a brother to Lyuda. His presence in any company was usually a guarantee of stability and sensible decisions.

Yuri Krivonishenko

Soon they received a letter from yet another Yuri, Yuri Krivonischenko, who had moved to Chelyabinsk, about 200 kilometres south, where he had a job as a physicist and engineer. He confirmed his participation. The whole of his letter was about the forthcoming expedition. It began with a romantic poem dedicated to those who love exploring the wilderness. The last line was: 'I can honestly say that I miss camp life a lot, and dream how great the expedition will be for me!'

Yuri joining the team made Lyuda very happy. Krivonischenko was fun and would be a kind of anchor for the rest. His friends often drank tea together at his parents' spacious apartment in the city centre. Krivonischenko's parents were well-educated and influential people, and they often welcomed students to their place. His father was the chief construction engineer of the Beloyarski Hydro-Electro Station. Yuri himself was the life of the party. He never let a single expedition happen without him.

Preparations appeared to be going well, but then some of the participants decided to pull out; and then a second problem arose in getting Rustem on the expedition at all. Rustem worked at a secret atomic plant, involved in producing plutonium for weapons. In order to include him on the expedition, the university sent an official letter to his place of work, but there was no answer.

By this time Lyuda was feeling desperate. It was at this moment that another person arrived on the scene. His name was Igor Dyatlov. Once he was involved, everything fell into place. He was a natural leader.

Igor Dyatlov

Hiking was Igor Dyatlov's one true love. In particular, he was passionate about the Ural Mountains.

The Urals are seldom compared to the Himalayas or the Alps: they are not seen as among the most dangerous mountains in the world, nor do they inspire modern climbers in terms of altitude or scale. The Urals have no major precipices, and few challenging crags. But they do have crevasses and magnetic anomalies which can throw a compass up to thirty percent off true.

As well as these hazards, nature has created a wind-tunnel between two particular mountain peaks: Kholat Syakhl and what was then called Peak 880, though on modern maps it is called 'innominate [unnamed] peak 905.4.' The first is shown on the map with an elevation of 1079m and the other is marked 880m. One would have to pass this tunnel in order to ascend onto the peak known as Otorten which, many believe, was sacred for the local ingenious people, the Mansi. The name 'Otorten' means 'Don't go there.'

This is exactly where Igor Dyatlov wanted to go. He liked breaking rules.

Dyatlov was neither tall nor muscular. He had a gap in his teeth, and was not especially good-looking. But there was something extremely charismatic about him. His passion for expeditions was almost maniacal. For him the mountains represented a journey into a world of freedom, a joyous relief from the grinding central control of the Communist Party. When he went on expeditions, it was he – not the Party – who was in charge. In the mountains he made his own decisions and was able to test his mettle and his independence.

At that time, Dyatlov was at the peak of his physical and athletic ability and was respected by the ski-hiking community in Sverdlovsk. According to Vadim Brusnitsin, a fellow student, 'We considered Igor to be the most experienced ski-hiker at the University.'

For them, 'ski-hiker' was the term they preferred for those who went on exciting adventures in the wintry, treacherous mountains.

A talented engineer, Dyatlov had already started to work at the UPI in research. Many girls liked him, but there was only one he liked in return. This girl was always laughing and talking fast. Her eyes were dark, lively, shining. Zina was a dynamo in the Explorer's Club. All the men in the group liked her.

Zina Kolmogorova

Zina herself wrote that wherever she appeared, people always said to her: 'Oh, you must be from around here. I must know you.' She had the most sociable character in the world. 'Everywhere she went, she filled the area with the pleasant breath of her soul,' Yudin, the only survivor of the expedition, recalled many years later.

Zina Kolmogorova had six expeditions under her belt already. Four were of the second category of complexity – an intermediate level – and she was a constant participant in expeditions organized by Dyatlov. Like Dyatlov himself, Zina was interested in radio and studied Radio Engineering at the UPI. The two were always seen together. A photo of her was found later in his notebook.

If she had any romantic feelings towards Igor, however, there's not the slightest clue in her personal letter to him (dated January 16, 1959) from Kamensk where, for the 'placement' part of her university course, she worked at a radio plant. In her letter, she only asks Igor to update her on how things were going with regard to the preparations for the expedition. But Igor was quite happy with her letter because he appreciated Zina's involvement. For him it was enough that she was going to participate. All his thoughts were about the adventure ahead of them. This would be his tenth expedition, and it would give him the right to win the qualification of Master, a rank equivalent to the rank of *Bergführer* in the European Alps.

It was only in 2004 that Zina's friend Valentina Tokareva shared a letter Zina wrote to her on the day of the expedition.

> My dearest Valya, here we are on our way to the expedition. Do you want a surprise? Yuri Doroshenko is coming with us. I really don't know how I'll feel. I relate to him like anyone else, but it's really hard, because we are together and yet we're not together.

Yuri Doroshenko, a fellow student, the tallest in the group and sometimes pictured with glasses, came from a very poor family. He usually wore a jacket inadequate to protect him from the freezing temperatures of Sverdlovsk. Very reserved, the twenty-one-year old hardly talked to the beautiful Zina when they had been on a previous expedition to Eastern Sayany.

Yuri Doroshenko

One day she was watching him putting up their tent on the edge of a forest when she noticed a large brown bear approaching. Zina let out a shout of alarm. In the next moment, she saw Yuri fearlessly advancing on the beast with only a geology hammer in his hand. He didn't pursue the animal for long, but when he strode back to the camp it was the moment Zina fell in love with him.

That night, they talked while making a campfire together. Doroshenko told her of his mother, who lived in Aktubinsk city in Kazakhstan, and who for several years had been saving money in order to buy him a warm coat. Zina told him of her home town, Kamensk-Uralsky and of her sister Tamara who was going to come over for New Year's Eve. They laughed as Zina recalled how their friends had gathered together for the last New Year's Eve celebration, and how, although they only had two bottles of champagne for about 50 people, they still had fun all night.

Following that conversation, the two often found themselves side by side, but neither Yuri nor Zina had any idea what an 'expedition pick-up' was. The girls routinely shared tents with the boys, and they would lay close to each other, talking. There was so much of life ahead, unexplored.

When they got back to Sverdlovsk they started to date. Yuri once visited Zina's home in Kamensk-Uralsky, where she introduced him to her family. He also had Zina's pictures at his home. After a while, something went wrong in the relationship. It was over by the time the Dyatlov expedition started. It was apparently Yuri who initiated the break.

Zina immersed herself completely in the preparation process. Together with Dyatlov she met up with Yevgeny Maslennikov, the head of the university's Explorer's Club. Dyatlov told him of the plan to organize a trek to the Urals, a trek they referred to as being of the 'third category' of difficulty, which meant the most challenging. They didn't discuss the route in detail at the time, but merely outlined the general idea of walking from Ivdel, a small town 535 kilometres north of Sverdlovsk and near the Ural range. Maslennikov supported the idea and soon the list of the participants, all experienced ski-hikers, was ready:

Alexander (Sasha) Kolevatov (24)

Rustem Slobodin (23)

Yuri (Georgi) Krivonischenko (23)

Yuri Doroshenko (21, but turned 22 on the sixth day of the trip)

Yuri Yudin (22)

Nicolai (Kolya) Thibeaux-Brignolles (Tibo) (23)

Alexander (Semyon) Zolotariov (the oldest at 37)

Lyuda Dubinina (20)

Zina Kolmogorova (22)

There were nine people in the expedition. All of them were friends and had been on several other expeditions together. All, that is, except one person whom no-one really knew...

# 3

Lyuda was checking her list against the pile of foods on the table in front of her. The door of University Room No. 531 was open and people were coming in and out all the time.

> Bread, crackers 7kg; oats and buckwheat 7kg; dry noodles 5kg; condensed milk in tins 2.5kg; preserved meat 4kg; butter, sausage 4kg; smoked pork 3kg; tea 200g; coffee 200g; cocoa 200g; dry milk, sugar.

As a head of provision distribution Lyuda had to make sure everything was included. These were austere and gloomy times in the Soviet Union. The Explorers Club was quite poor financially and members could only take fairly basic staples with them. The smoked pork was a special gift from the University for this occasion.

> 'We forgot the salt! Three kilograms! Igor! Where are you? Where is Doroshenko? Why did he take twenty packs?'

The room was a mess. Yuri Krivonischenko and Rustem Slobodin were frantically shoving cans and tins into backpacks. The single large, old tent was still to be packed.

> 'Can't fit it. Damn. Who has the knife?'
> 'Yuri drove it to the station.'
> 'Lyuda, give me fifteen kopeks.'
> 'Where are my felt boots?'

There was a certain informality about their preparations. They took no radio with them. From our modern viewpoint this seems reckless, but it was impossible to buy a walkie-talkie in the USSR in the late 1950s. The only portable radio readily available to members of the public (as opposed to the military) weighed 40 kilograms – hardly practical for a trip to the shops, let alone up a mountain.

Dyatlov, however, was a talented radio hobbyist. He was a registered radio operator with his own identifying call sign, and had even made his own primitive analogue walkie-talkie in 1956, which he used on an expedition the next year. He had a radio set, which was kept in the Climbing Club, a subdivision of the university's Explorer's Club. No one knows why he didn't take it on the expedition.

Lyuda gave everyone a notebook to use as a diary. Keeping an expedition log was a daily duty, a trademark even, of the Explorer's Club. There was also one general diary, in which every member could write. Some entries consisted of single words or short phrases, shorthand reminders of their trip for later, understood only by the writer.

By the time they were ready to depart for the railway station, Igor Dyatlov unexpectedly introduced them to a rather unusual man, with the appearance of someone from Caucasus. The man's name was Semyon Zolotariov. Dyatlov said: 'He wants to go on the expedition with us.' The man flashed his metal teeth and said: 'Just call me Sasha for short.'

Lyuda didn't like the fact that Zolotariov was much older than the rest of them. He was also single, which was odd for a Russian man of 37. On the day of their meeting, she wrote in her diary:

> At first, no one wanted him in the group because he's completely new to us, but then we got over it and he's here. We couldn't just refuse to take him.

Alexander (Semyon) Zolotariov

Everyone knew that the inclusion of this 'dark horse' in the group had been orchestrated by the local Communist Party Committee. Fellow student Valentin Bogomolov recalls how eager Zolotariov was to finish the trek as soon as possible, giving the impression he was in a big hurry to perform some other duty once it had been completed.

Zolotariov, however, willingly shared some facts about himself with the rest of the group. He had been awarded four medals during the Second World War, and had hoped to continue in the military afterwards; but instead he re-trained in sports at the Minsk Institute of Physical Education (GIFKB) and now worked as a tour guide.

Zolotariov made Lyuda uneasy: she suspected that he felt used to being in charge, and wondered if that might be a problem. The fact that the group now included one leader aged 23 and one aged 37 could make for some tension.

There were two UPI student groups leaving Sverdlovsk on the same day. One was Dyatlov's group, and another was led by a student named Yuri Blinov. His was also a mixed-sex group. The two groups started the trip together but subsequently parted to go their own separate ways.

Just before our departure, those who wanted to say goodbye came to meet us. We were really short of time, but arrived at the railway station with seconds to spare. Then we had to say goodbye to everyone.

(From Lyuda Dubinina's personal diary, January 23, 1959)

# 4

It has been said that if Hitler or Napoleon had ever taken a train from Moscow to Siberia they would have promptly abandoned any idea of conquering Russia. The winter view out of the window of the train is one of endless, unrelieved forest and snow with hardly any habitation. Occasionally a trace of smoke from a small forest hut can be seen before the great forest, known as the taiga, again overwhelms the eyes. The taiga is enormous, wild, unrelenting and dangerous. It has been said to break hearts. The snow there can be three meters deep in the harshest of winters, and temperatures can easily reach minus 40 degrees Celsius. It is difficult for most to understand why people explore this wilderness, test themselves in it, or live in it.

On January 23, 1959, Zina wrote in her diary:

And here we are on the train. We sang all the songs we know, learned new ones, everyone is going to sleep at 3 AM. I wonder what awaits us on this trip. The boys solemnly swore not to smoke for the entire trip. I wonder how much willpower they have, and if they can get by without cigarettes? Everyone is on the verge of falling asleep and the Ural taiga spreads out in all directions.

Their arrival in the town of Serov the following morning was marked by an unpromising incident: Yuri Krivonischenko was detained by the police at the railway station. At first the police did not let the group into the building. They probably thought these young people were too noisy for the sleepy settlement, but then they relented and allowed the group to enter the station. Krivonischenko was great fun to be around, and on that morning he was in a particularly exuberant mood. First he asked Lyuda for money to buy breakfast in a café. Lyuda, who was the group's treasurer, told him they couldn't afford it. Perhaps she was trying to compensate for her extravagance in Sverdlovsk, where she'd bought that unnecessary five metres of cambric which cost 200 roubles. In response, Krivonischenko started to sing loudly, and the police were swiftly alerted. But Krivonischenko was not only singing when he was approached by the policeman: he was also acting like a panhandler, walking around with a hat in his hands and asking for money. 'They immediately took him to the police station. The policeman told him singing in public places is forbidden. This is the first public place where it's forbidden to sing!'

Lyuda tried to find an explanation as to why the police took this approach. 'It's because this town is very calm, as if it's already a Communist era here – no crime, no law violations – and then our Yurka Krivonischenko started to sing loudly.'

The group spent a full day waiting in Serov for the next train. They were welcomed at a nearby secondary school where they were given the chance to warm up and to use the hot water, and in return they talked to the kids about trekking. Yudin wrote:

> We spent two hours lecturing and the kids didn't want to let us go. At the bus station we saw the whole school. In the end, as we were leaving, the kids yelled and cried, asking Zina to remain with them. They promised to listen to her and study well.

The group then took another train to Ivdel, which is surrounded by a complex of prison camps, the *Ivdelag*. Even today, the town still mainly serves the needs of prisoners and those who work in the prisons. And again the journey was nothing but fun. Lyuda wrote:

We sang and sang, and no one even noticed how we started to discuss love issues, talking about kisses in particular. We talked all kinds of nonsense, of course; everyone was interested, everyone wanted to speak out, eventually trying to out-shout each other and prove their own opinion. Sasha Kolevatov was the best in our debates. Probably he expressed not only his own thoughts but, anyway, he obviously won.

Alexander Kolevatov

It's no wonder Alexander Kolevatov won. He wasn't like the simple people of Sverdlovsk; he'd lived and worked in Moscow for three years. 'Sasha' Kolevatov smoked a pipe with good tobacco and was always very tidy. He was the last cherished child of a couple with four daughters, who were eager to have a boy. Their dream came true in 1934 when his mother was already forty. Unfortunately, his father died when Kolevatov was only ten.

Kolevatov proved to be very bright, and though he went to a very ordinary college in Sverdlovsk, he earned himself a prestigious, well-paid job in Moscow, with which he was able to support his elderly, now handicapped, mother.

Russian people generally tend to relocate from a province to the capital, not the other way around, so it was a rather strange move to leave this interesting and lucrative job and return to Sverdlovsk. It was well known by the other members of the group that Kolevatov wrote his diary meticulously and accurately on every expedition, and tried to keep it strictly private.

That conversation about love and kisses made Zina feel a bit elegiac. In her next letter to Valentina she wrote:

> What should you do if you feel sad? You have to go on. Right? If you only see the good things in life, then you'll get more joy out of it. Everything will be fine, I promise. (I feel very sad today because he's walking around holding hands with one of the girls. I'm jealous.)

Doroshenko was holding the hand of one of the girls in Blinov's group but, with only one more collective bus trip to make, from Ivdel to Vizhay, the two groups would soon part and continue on their separate routes.

Trying to amuse herself by reading, Zina focused on learning more about the Mansi, the indigenous people that live in the Urals region. She found out that their language, Mansi, is an Ugrian language of the Uralic family. She also discovered that the name of the peak Otorten was *Woot-Taaratane-Syachl*, which means 'a mountain producing wind', or more simply and neatly 'a windy mountain.'

But other researchers said this name was associated by mistake with Peak 880. The Mansi name for Peak 1079 was *Lunt-Choosup-Syachl*, meaning 'Mount Goose Nest'. There was a Mansi legend that, after the global flood, one goose survived on the peak of this mountain. What Zina tried to understand, reading the book of a native Mansi linguist, Tatiana Slinkina, was whether Otorten really meant 'Don't go there', as many believed.

She could not find any confirmation. There was no proof of a second legend that nine Mansi people once disappeared there. This was good to know for a member of an expedition also numbering nine.

But Slinkina added some unsettling information nevertheless: 'The Mansi always try to avoid *Woot-Taaratane-Syachl* and *Lunt-Choosup- Syachl,* especially the "gates" between them. They have considered them sacred and dangerous since ancient times.'

The author offered no explanation why.

There was a young man among the Dyatlov's group who would never have been there in that remote region at all, if his great grandfather hadn't moved to Russia at the end of the eighteenth century. He was Nicolai Thibeaux-Bringnolle, known as Tibo, whose Russian-French name was conspicuous in Russia for its rarity.

His great-grandfather, a French mechanic, had settled in Saint Petersburg. One of his sons had become a fairly well-known architect, but fate was not so kind to his grandson, Tibo's father, who worked as a mining engineer in the Sverdlovsk region, ended up in one of Stalin's camps as an 'enemy of the people.

Despite a childhood overshadowed by his father's imprisonment and death, Tibo grew up to be a friendly man with a good sense of humour, intelligent and fun to be around. In order to avoid the stigma of being the son of an 'enemy of the people', as well as to justify his imperialistic last name, he created a legend that his ancestor was a French communist.

It's also Tibo who should be credited for supplying his friends with certain books, essential for those times, such as *The Sexual Question* by Auguste Forel. The following is his record for January 26, 1959 made in Vizhay:

Nicolai Thibeaux-Bringnolle

We slept in a so-called hotel. Two people per bed. Sasha K. [Alexander Kolevatov] and Krivoy [Yuri Krivonischenko] slept on the floor between the beds. Woke up at 9 AM. Everyone slept well despite the fact that we didn't completely close the small window and the room got a bit cold. Outside, the temperature is −17C. We didn't brew our tea in the morning, the wood was damp; in the evening it took us six hours to boil water. Went to lunch in the dining room. Then they served cold tea and Igor Dyatlov said with a sarcastic smile: 'If the tea is cold, then go out and drink it on the street, and it will be hot.' What a clever idea!

It isn't clear to whom Dyatlov addressed his sarcasm. It may have been Tibo, but he was easy-going and not easily offended.

In Vizhay they went to a cinema, and were impressed with the movie. Afterwards they talked a lot. Lyuda:

We are extremely lucky! The Golden Symphony was showing. We left all our things and packs at the hotel and went to the club. The image was a bit fuzzy, but it didn't overshadow the pleasure at all. Yurka Krivo, sitting next to me, was smacking his lips and oohing with delight. This is real happiness, so difficult to describe with words. The music is just fabulous! We loved the movie. Even Igor Dyatlov let his hair down. He tried to dance, and even started singing.

Dyatlov's group on their way from Vizhay

Dyatlov's group left the following day in high spirits. From Vizhay, they travelled north towards the mysterious peak, Otorten, which dominated this part of the Urals.

For the next stage of the trip, from Vizhay to a logging community called Settlement 41, the Dyatlov group hitched a ride. Describing their arrival, Lyuda wrote at length:

At 4.30 we were warmly welcomed, and stayed in a cabin where the men lived. Everyone living here are freelance workers. There were no women at all, save two. As Igor admitted, all the men were young, and some of them even handsome and smart. The most prominent of all was a red-bearded man called Ognev. He was dubbed 'Beard.' It's so lucky to meet a person like that in such a hole. He was a true adventurer, geologist and a very smart fellow. We broke into two groups: some watched movies, the others filled in their diaries. Meanwhile, Rustem and Kolya talked about this and that, about the job and so on. I like these two guys! I have to admit, there's a noticeable gap between the people who graduated (Rustem, Ko and Yuri) and the rest of us. Their speculations are much smarter and more mature than ours. Gosh, to say nothing of mine.

Everyone felt really tired after the movie and wanted to sleep. Zina and I lay on a mesh-work bed. It's a dream. The lads rested right on the floor. The mood is horrible. Seems it's going to be horrible for about two more days. I'm mad as a devil.


Judging from the last lines, it appears that the high spirits of the previous day had evaporated, possibly because those who'd given up smoking were beginning to experience withdrawal and were getting snappy.

Why was Lyuda 'mad,' and her mood disconsolate? There's no direct explanation, but, from her diary entries, we might guess that the cause of her general discontent could be due to relations with the opposite sex: we read several times that she's not happy with the way she talks to others (mostly men). She scolds herself for the things she says, and even for her own ideas about life. She imagines that Zinoviev considers her 'foolish' … all this while Zina has no problem; always appreciated by men, always laughing and always the centre of attention. For this reason, every trifle or word could make Lyuda feel angry or sad.

I sometimes wonder if she was able to anticipate tragedy, and felt oppressed because she unconsciously sensed the approach of something terrible. Perhaps this is the reason she stopped keeping her diary on January 28.

# 5

*Kholat Syakhl* doesn't exactly mean the 'Mountain of the Dead,' as is so often claimed, rather it means *The Dead Mountain*. According to scientists this gloomy name was given to it because no plants grew on its slopes. It's like the Dead Sea, which, after all, we don't call the 'Sea of the Dead.'

But nine young people who were on their way to that place didn't think of such things. On the evening of January 26, Zina wrote: 'I put Yuri's mittens on today, though I was reluctant to do so. But the guys told me I was wrong, and so I did put them on. Talking to each other. Just a bit.'

When Doroshenko considerately offered Zina his mittens to warm her hands, she initially refused them, since he was no longer her boyfriend and she didn't want any such care from him – a normal reaction from a Russian girl, who wants all or nothing from the man she still has in her heart. Her friends, however, made her aware that this kind of behaviour was not appropriate on an expedition where personal matters shouldn't affect one's decisions. So she accepted the mittens and even tried to talk to him, though it was not easy for her.

It's unlikely that Yuri Doroshenko wrote any of this in the notebook he was given by Lyuda; it was more usually the girls who wrote about their feelings. But it was he who added the next page in the communal diary on January 27:

> The weather's really good. The wind is at our backs, and the lads made a deal with the locals for a horse to drive us to Second Severny settlement. But it will be about 24 km (14 mi) from the 41st Settlement. We helped Uncle Slava unload hay from a carriage and waited for the horse (it went to get more hay and wood). We waited until 4:00 PM. The

boys started copying some songs. One man sang beautifully. We heard a number of illegal prison songs (Article 58 counter-revolutionary crimes).

Yuri went on to talk about travel to their next stop:

Ognev told Igor how to find a house where we can spend the night. We bought four loaves of bread and arrived at 4:00 PM. Soft warm bread. Ate two pieces. The horse is slow. What a pleasure to go without our backpacks. We covered 8 km (5 mi) in two hours. (Ushma River). It gets darker. All the delay is due to the horse. Yuri Yudin is riding with us. He suddenly fell ill and can't continue on the path. He wants to gather a few local minerals for the university and return.

Yudin shortly before leaving the group

Though the decision to leave was only made on January 27, Yuri Yudin, a fourth-year student in the Engineering and Economics Department of UPI, actually left the group the following day. Yuri was an old friend of the whole team. Some think that, if he hadn't left the group at this point, everything might have been different. This was even stated later by the star of a Russian national TV show about people with paranormal abilities, Dmitry Volkov.

Zina was, of course, sorry when Yudin left. 'Yuri Yudin is leaving us today – it's such a pity, really, but he's got sciatica and has to leave. His stuff was put into our backpacks.'

She goes on to say:

It [leaving Settlement 41] means this is the last time we see other people, and any signs of civilization.

Lyuda and I slept on a bed for the last time last night. Apparently, next time it will be the tent. We are in Settlement 41 now; our aim is to reach the Second Severny mining camp today. People say we'll find an empty house where no one lives. I wish we were moving already! And skis of course.

I wonder how we'll do with the skiing.

She later adds:

We walked along the Lozva River all day, with horses ahead and behind us. We went through ice fields pretty often, and had to clean our skis. We arrived late at night and spent a lot of time looking for a house with windows and doors.

The Second Severny mining camp is deserted, there's not a single soul here, but the scenery is just marvellous!

The Second Severny mining camp had once been filled with geologists and miners, but now over two thousand homes lay abandoned and empty, all uninhabitable apart from the one the group searched for. It was only a temporary settlement for the miners. They seem to have passed that night happily enough, making jokes, talking and playing 'dare' until the small hours of the morning.

The man with the horse sledge, who had accompanied them the previous day and carried their backpacks, was Lithuanian exile Velikyavichus (called 'Uncle Slava' by Yuri in the group diary). He stayed with them the night of January 27th, then returned to Settlement 41 the following day, taking with him Yudin's backpack containing the minerals he'd picked up. From the photos of the group's last goodbyes with Yudin, recovered from the cameras in their tattered tent, it's obvious they were fond of him and he'd be missed. Yudin returned to Settlement 41 on skis, while his friends went deeper into the taiga...

Walking along the Lozva River with a horse sledge

# 6

January 28, 1959.

We go up the Lozva River. Often we have to stop and scrape the wet, melting snow from the skis. Yuri Kri is behind and makes sketches of the route. We pass a few cliffs on the right bank of the Lozva River. Overall, the terrain becomes flatter. We stop at 5:30 PM. Today we spend our first night in the tent. The guys are busy with the furnace. With some things completed and others not, we sit for dinner. Once we're done, we make our way inside the tent. Nobody wants to sleep by the furnace and we agreed that Yuri Kri will sleep there. After two minutes Yuri moves to another place with terrible cursing and the accusation we betrayed him. We can't fall asleep for a while and argue about something.

(Unattributed diary entry)

Zina wrote the same day:

> The guys were joking and saying silly things yester-day in the evening. I think we shouldn't pay any attention to them. That will probably stop them from being so rude. Nothing else. It's time to depart, but they're still rooting around. How can they be such slow coaches? Sasha Kolev-atov was testing his device, then quit. A second halt. It was much easier yesterday to walk without the backpacks.

> Snow, snow, snow, snow has frozen along the banks of rivers, snow, snow. The snow is blowing. Lunch was at four. After lunch we made only one passage, then stopped for a halt. I mended the tent. Everyone went to sleep. Igor was rude throughout the whole evening. I just couldn't re-cognize him! I decided to sleep on the wood by the stove.

Again, Igor's uncharacteristic behaviour may have been due to nicotine withdrawal: he had gone for nearly five days without a cigarette. Presumably, they didn't take cigarettes with them, so they couldn't have smoked even if they'd wanted to. Tibo's entry for the following day, January 29, is brief:

Second day of our hike. We made our way from the Lozva River to the Auspiya River. We walked along a Mansi trail. The weather is –13C (8F). The wind is weak. We often find ice on the Lozva River. That is it.

Tibo, Zolotariov, Slobodin and Dubinina

Zina's entry is equally brief, and includes observations about the Mansi trail. She was obviously working things out with Yuri now. 'Yuri and I were discussing the past while sawing the firewood. He's such a playboy.'

January 30 [no attribution]: The diary is written in the cold on the go. Today's the third cold night on the shore of the Auspiya River. The stove does a great job. Some (Tibo and Krivonischenko) think we need to construct a heating system in the tent. Having curtains hung in the tent is quite justified. We get up at 8:30 AM. After breakfast we walk along the Auspiya River, but again these ice dams don't allow us to move forward. Let's go to the shore of the sledge-deer trail. In the middle of the road we discovered markings left by the Mansi.

We were walking along the Auspiya [River] all day long. We will probably construct a 'labaz' today.

Starting a new day. Jan. 30, 1959

The 'labaz' referred to is a platform raised off the ground, on which a supply of food is stored for the return journey to keep it safe. This would also have lightened the load in their backpacks, so they didn't have so much to carry as they climbed higher over the next few days. Igor Dyatlov planned to make a traverse on the lower northern slopes of Mountain 1079, and then along the ridge of Poyasovy, taking advantage of the firm snow, before retracing their route back the same way. This route would have permitted a very easy descent from the ridge to the wooded valley of the Lozva River, where they could find a good spot to set up camp and make use of the furnace. This radial path could have been completed in three days.

The entire length of the planned route was 180 km (112 mi). The goal was to be back in Vizhay by February 12 and then in Sverdlovsk a couple of days later, on about February 14 or 15. An alternative route might have been from the storage depot up to the Poyasovy crag and its slope, and then to continue moving in a southerly direction to another mountain, *Oika-Chakour*. This was the most southerly point of the whole route, from which they could go east back to Vizhay, and from where they had promised to send a telegram. No telegram ever arrived, and the very last record in the diary is made by Dyatlov himself on January 31:

The weather's a bit worse today: the wind is blowing (westerly), it's surprisingly snowing (probably the snow falling from trees) though the sky is completely clear.

We started relatively early (about 10 AM). We're walking along the Mansi ski-track. (Up to now we've been moving along the recent track of a Mansi hunter who must've been riding a reindeer.) I think it was his overnight shelter we saw yesterday. The deer must've stopped there, while the hunter himself continued along the old trail. We're following in his track now.

Last night was surprisingly nice: it was rather warm and dry despite the low temperature (–18 to –24C/0 to – 10 F). It's especially difficult to walk today. No traces are seen, we miss the way pretty often and have to move almost gropingly. Thus, we manage to walk at a pace of about 1.52 kph (0.630 mph).

We are trying to invent new methods of skiing: the first person takes his backpack off and walks for 5 minutes, then returns, rests for about 10-15 minutes and catches up with the rest of the group. Thus a method of non-stop ski-track making was created. The second person moving after the first, but with a pack on his back, has the most difficult task.

We're gradually leaving the Auspiya. The ascent is continuous but rather smooth. We passed fir trees and found ourselves in a rare birch forest. Then we reached the forest edge. The wind is westerly, warm and blistering, with the same impression of air speed as when a plane is taking off. There is ice crust everywhere around us. The making of a storage depot is not feasible at all. It's about 4 PM.

We need to find somewhere suitable to camp for the night. We're going down to the Auspiya Valley. It seems to be the snowiest place here. The wind is slack, the snow is 1.22 m (3.28 ft) deep. Tired and exhausted we started to prepare the place for the overnight stop. We lacked firewood, which consisted mostly of weak, wet fir trees. We made a fire on logs – no one wanted to dig a special hole for it. We had dinner right in the tent. It's warm in here. It's difficult to imagine such comfort somewhere on a mountain range with the severe howl of the wind hundreds of kilometres from any inhabited places.

Then there was nothing but silence.

# PART II: THE SEARCH

# 1

Back then, in 1959, Yekaterinburg was known as Sverdlovsk. The original name was changed from Yekaterinburg to Sverdlovsk in 1926, and then at the time of Gorbachev's *perestroika* in 1991, back again to Yekaterinburg.

It is also the city where the last Russian Czar, Nicolas II, and his family were arrested and killed. And at the end of the eighteenth century, it became a gold-rush city and gold fever turned this region into a developed territory.

Also, Yekaterinburg is where the American pilot Francis Gary Powers was shot down on May 1, 1960 while performing secret aerial reconnaissance.

During the Second World War, the city was the main military production centre for the Soviet Union, and many armament factories were located there. Half of all the tanks used by the Soviet Union in the war had rolled onto their transports from Yekaterinburg's factory gates. In fact, since its very origins in the seventeenth century, Yekaterinburg has been one of Russia's main industrial cities. The city's metallurgical production in the eighteenth century was the greatest in Europe. After the 1917 revolution, the Soviets endeavoured to construct the country's largest factory for heavy machinery, called *Uralmash. Uralmash* was a leading European metropolis in its own right, occupying a site as large as any self-respecting city.

It was Kolevatov's eldest sister, Rimma, who was very fond of her brother, who first realised something had gone wrong with the expedition and alerted the whole city. As news of a missing group of students spread throughout Sverdlovsk, an uproar began to sweep the place. The idea that talented, charismatic, healthy young people had been lost in the north, on mountains that were not perceived as particularly dangerous, was a great shock for the city, so proud of its proximity to the stunningly beautiful Urals.

The following is based on the extensive records of those involved, and is a timeline of events immediately after the alarm was raised. The group failed to arrive in Vizhay on February 12 but, as noted by Yuri Yudin at the time, they'd most likely lost a day due to carrying the extra load he'd left them with upon turning back. Yet, by February 17 there was still no trace of the group.

Soon, worried parents started to call the university Sports Club asking for news. Some even queried the Communist Party's local office. Later, trying to comprehend the tragedy, Rimma asked many questions no one wanted to answer.

On February 20, the Explorer's Club of the university called a meeting, and the other expedition groups were informed that there might be a problem. The participants were swiftly organized into search parties, including the hikers from groups that had recently returned. The groups led by Sergey Sogrin, Yuri Blinov, and Vladislav Karelin all received telegrams telling them to stop and wait for reinforcements.

### February 21

More teams from the university were dispatched to help with the search. One team was led by Boris Slobtsov, a student at the UPI, another by Oleg Grebenik, also a UPI student, and the third by Moses Axelrod, an experienced climber. Under the command of Captain Alexey Chernyshov, a fourth fresh group comprising military personnel was dispatched. Some local Mansi people were also asked to help.

Moscow was made aware of the incident, and soon also sent a few experienced hikers. Yevgeny Maslennikov, the head of the university's Explorer's Club, was appointed to coordinate the search, together with Colonel George Ortykov of the Army, who was in charge of overall logistics and helicopter support. Within hours, the first student groups were dropped at strategic points, and Boris Slobtsov's team was placed on Mount 1055.

In Slobtsov's group were Vadim Brusnitsin, Yuri Koptelov, Vladimir Lebedev, and Mikhail Sharavin, and others. At the time of writing, all of them are still alive and have shared their memories of the events. Local hunter guides Ivan Pashin and Alex Cherglakov also took part in the search.

*February 24*

Within five hours of the aerial search, a ski trail was spotted running along the bank of the Auspiya River and then in the direction of the ridge. The trail appeared to be old.

Boris Slobtsov (central)

Slobtsov wrote:

On the top, where we were brought in by helicopter, we saw no tracks. The next day was dedicated to some useless searches along the Lozva River. That very day we came to the banks of the Auspiya, where we knew that Dyatlov was intending to create his storage depot. Sure enough, on

47

the left bank of this river we found some old ski tracks. A radio message was sent by our search team operator, and we received the following message from our fellow rescue group: 'We're six or ten kilometres from the Auspiya and we've found narrow sports ski tracks, different to the wide tracks of the Mansi skis. It's a good trail made by a number of people, and is probably 10-15 days old, very easy to follow in the forest, but almost invisible in open places. The track goes to the ridge, where of course it disappears due to wind and snow drifts.'

*February 26*

The rescuers worked hard to try to identify where the group had left the river valley. Some groups looked for tracks, whilst others sought the storage depot.

On February 26, Boris Slobtsov and Michael Sharavin, together with Ivan Pashin the local guide, arrived at a pass between the two rivers. Slobtsov said the guide 'tried to convince us that the entire group had fallen into a crevasse somewhere close to Mount Otorten, but it was obvious that he himself didn't want to proceed.

As they were skiing towards Otorten, they noticed the dark shape of a tent covered by snow and a protruding stovepipe on the slope of the Kholat Syakhl. Pashin refused to approach the tent, so the two students went on alone. Upon encountering the scene, they noted:

The tent was situated on the northeast slope of the Kholat Syakhl Mountain. It was about 300 metres (980 ft) from the summit and was pitched on a special flat area dug into the snow, with some snow walls around it for protection from the wind. One end of the tent faced southeast towards the Auspiya River, the other faced northwest towards the Lozva River.

Another rescue team member described the slope as 'uneven and descending, and crossed by three stony ridges parallel to one another before passing into a hollow'.

'As we approached the tent, we discovered the entrance was out of the snow, but the rest was buried. In the snow around the tent, there were ski poles and one pair of skis. The snow on the tent was 15-20 cm (5-7.5") deep. The snow had obviously drifted there and was very firm. At the side of the tent there was a Chinese flashlight, which we later found belonged to Dyatlov. But we couldn't understand why the snow under the flashlight was ten centimetres thick, yet there wasn't any on the flashlight itself. I put the flashlight down and saw it was switched off. I switched it on and there was light. I didn't notice it at the time, but I was later told that close to the side of the tent was a mark where someone had urinated, and next to the entrance of the tent was an ice-pick.'

The tent partly cleared of the snow. The men are Yuri Koptelov and Vladislav Karelin. Photo by V. Brusnitsin, Feb 27, 1959

There were no bodies near the tent or inside it. The students took the diaries and a flask of alcohol from the tent before returning to join the rest of the group. Around 4PM that day, they met another group with a radio set and sent a message with the co-ordinates of the tent.

*February 27*
Maslennikov himself arrived at the tent and started to inspect it with great and meticulous care. He later recorded in files used in the subsequent criminal case:

"At first sight, the tent appeared to be covered with snow but, when we looked closer, we saw it was still pitched on its pole at the entrance and was held firmly by the guy-ropes. A stick held the other end, but the middle sagged from the weight of the snow, and the windward side was shredded and torn apart, so the other end was low and buried in snow.

It wasn't possible to observe the interior until we'd dug it out, but the tent was well placed and they'd used their upturned skis as a flat floor below the ground sheet. A stove lay next to the entrance of the tent, but it was disassembled and in [its] cover. There was a single log outside the tent.

We also noticed, almost all their things were in place: a bucket, axes, and cups."

In his later testimony, Sharavin added that the stove was full of unburnt wood.

A more detailed account of the cuts and tears of the tent can be found in the chapter devoted to the criminal case file, but at this point it should be noted that Sharavin later said he also made a hole on the ridge of the tent with an ice pick and then tore the tent horizontally. Because the rescue team was in shock and hadn't even considered that their fellow students could be dead, they didn't treat the crime scene with proper care, nor did they preserve all the evidence for the investigation.

Personal testimonies from all members of the rescue teams are available in the criminal case records; however, as might be expected with so many witnesses, they didn't report on the same things.

Atmanaki: 'There was a roll of film 15 metres (50 ft) below the tent. It probably came from inside the tent, when we spread out the things we found inside to study them.'

Vadim Brusnitsin stated, 'While we worked there, we tried to remove the snow using other skis and ski poles. There were ten of us working without any system. Often we just took stuff out of the snow and it was hard to say what came from where.'

The official report from the criminal investigation states:
The belongings inside were situated as follows:
By the entrance was a furnace; baskets; water flasks, one of which was filled with alcohol; a saw; and an axe. Deeper inside were the cameras. Further back was a bag with maps and documents, Dyatlov's camera, a can containing money, Kolmogorova's diary and windbreakers belonging to Dyatlov and Kolevatov. In the corner was a bag of rusks and another bag containing breakfast cereal. Next to them was a pair of boots. The other six pairs of boots were at the opposite side of the tent. In the middle of the tent were three pairs of *valenki* [footwear] and one single one. Next to the rusks there was a log taken from the place of the previous camp. Above all, there was a ski pole, scored at several places.

In the opinion of one of the members of the search party, 'They would only have spoiled the ski pole under emergency conditions, because they had no spares.'

Maslennikov added in his report to the court: 'When we finished taking inventory of the tent's contents, we moved it to the helicopter pad, about 600-700 metres (0.3-0.4 mi) away.'

The search team sent a radio message, stating: 'We managed to identify footprints of eight or nine people starting from the tent and going about one kilometre down the slope, and then they were lost. One person was in boots, the others were only in socks and barefoot.'

Some members of the rescue team claimed these footprints started from right outside the tent, and others that they started a little to the side of the tent.

Atmanaki: 'There were no footprints right around the tent because when the Dyatlov group dug they had stacked the snow all around, and later this snow was drifted by the wind, thus covering all the tracks. But thirty or forty metres down there was a file of very well-preserved footprints.'

Slobtsov's statement, taken from the criminal case file, is as follows: 'There were footprints of bare feet, but in socks. Some were from valenki, and occasionally we could make out the tread of a ski boot. All of these prints were raised higher than the actual wind-scoured surface of the slope. We followed these prints from the tent in the direction of a spreading cedar, which was clearly prominent on the hill. First we lost, and then we found, the tracks again. They appeared again in the birch-tree undergrowth, and then they went down along the ravine which led to the Lozva River.'

Brusnitsin's statement (again taken from the criminal case) explains the raised footprints: 'Footprints can be preserved in the mountains because of the way the wind works there. You see the prints not as lowered imprints, but rather as raised columns, because the snow under the print is left compacted and cannot be eroded by the wind, but the area around it is scoured by the wind. Then the sunrise makes the print area become even firmer, and in this way it can be preserved for the entire winter.'

Elevated footprints

Captain Chernyshov (testimony for the criminal case):
'Then they crossed a stony ridge where the tracks disappeared, but further down they appeared again, and then they were lost. The prints were very distinct. In some of the prints one could see whether the person was barefoot or in socks because you could see the toes.'

At about eleven in the morning, at a distance of about 1.5 km (0.620 mi) from the tent, Koptelov and Sharavin found the first two bodies.

# 2

The bodies were of Yuri Doroshenko and Yuri Krivonischenko. Neither Sharavin nor Koptelov were questioned during the investigation. Sharavin says that, by the time the investigation was conducted, he was in a hospital and therefore couldn't testify; even more reason why there should have been a statement by Koptelov. The statement in the criminal files is by Slobtsov:

'While looking carefully around the area, Mikhail (Sharavin) noticed something dark close to a cedar tree. There was a flat area next to the cedar, and on this were remains of a fire. About two or three metres from the fire they found Yuri Doroshenko, frozen without his clothes and with his hand burned; and a little to the side they found Yuri Krivonischenko in the same state. Under Doroshenko's body were three or four cedar branches of about the same thickness.'

Krivonischenko and Doroshenko's bodies partly cleared of the snow

Describing the condition of the bodies in the official record, Vasily Tempalov, the prosecutor in the criminal case, stated:

'Krivonischenko's right leg has no footwear. On his left foot there is a brown sock, torn. Another sock like this was discovered half burnt next to the fire. On the backs of his hands the skin is torn. Between the fingers there is blood. The index finger is also torn. The skin of the left shin is torn and covered in blood. There are no more visible injuries on his body.

Doroshenko has woollen socks on his feet, and over these socks another lighter sock. His ear, lips and nose are covered in blood, and on his left hand, the middle finger is bloody.'

At the time, however, it wasn't obvious that one of the corpses was Doroshenko's. Ortykov reported in the radio message sent by the search team to Ivdel, 'His face is completely covered in snow but we're now of the opinion he is Doroshenko, not Zolotariov. They are both the biggest guys.'

A student in the search party, Vadim Brusnitsin, made a statement for the criminal case: 'Next to the bodies was a fire. Nearby were more than ten small fir-tree branches, cut with a Finnish knife. The lower dry branches, of about 5-cm (1.32") diameter, had been cut from the cedar. Some of these were lying next to the fire. The snow around was trampled.'

From Captain Chernyshov's official statement: 'It's possible to surmise that other people had since been by the fire. We found various garments next to it rather than on the bodies, but we didn't find any other bodies. The trees near the fire had been cut with knives, but we found no knives with the bodies.'

Maslennikov stated that Doroshenko and Krivonischenko, 'maybe with the help of others, had made a pretty good fire with the branches of fir-trees. But that fire had been alight for maybe an hour and a half (8-cm/3.5" branches of cedar had burned through).'

Atmanaki stated for the criminal case: 'For about 20 metres (65 ft) around the cedar, there was evidence of young fir-trees being cut with a knife. We saw around 20 such cut stumps. But we didn't see any of the cut branches left, except for one. It isn't possible to imagine they were used to maintain the fire. First of all, they are not good for firewood. Second, around them were quite a lot of dry twigs and materials.'

The search team sent another radio message in which they stated that 'the volume of work done here in making this number of cuts suggests there were more people here than only these two.'

Maslennikov: 'Several wool and cotton socks were scattered around the fire. There was a woman's handkerchief burned through in several places and some fragments of woollen clothes. But we didn't find the actual clothes themselves. In particular, we found the cuff of a dark sweater there, not on the bodies. Also, we found some money, eight rubles.'

The tall cedar tree, originally spotted by Yury Koptelov and Mikhail Scharavin, held some clues to the events of that night. The following accounts from individuals present at the scene are similar and they bear each other out:

Captain Chernyshov:

'All the low branches of the cedar within arm's reach were broken completely. One was cut 4 or 5 m (13-16ft) high. They were thick. These types of branches are extremely difficult to break, even if, for instance, you hang on them with the whole weight of your body.'

Maslennikov:

'The lower dry branches of the cedar were broken up to 2 m (6.5ft) high. Somebody climbed the tree, because the branches four or five metres high were also broken.'

Dyatlov's body partly cleared of the snow

Atmanaki:

'Most of the dry branches up to five metres were broken. Beside this, the side of the tree facing the slope and the tent was completely cleared of branches. These were not dry; they were young and were not used. Some of them were just lying on the ground, and the others were hanging on the lower branches of the cedar. It looked as if someone had created a viewing hide facing the site from where they came.'

The same day, at a distance of 1100 m (0.7 mi) from the tent and 300 m (984 ft) from the cedar, Igor Dyatlov's body was found. He was lying on his back, his head in the direction of the tent, with no hat, covered with snow, and with his arm leaning on a small birch sapling.

Maslennikov:

'Dyatlov was lying 300 m away from the cedar towards the tent, next to a birch [sapling] with his face up. His left hand was kind of dragged to his face as if he had tried to protect himself from the wind. He was dressed more warmly than Doroshenko and

Krivonischenko. He had a fur vest, his collared shirt, underwear, ski trousers and other clothes. But he had no hat, gloves, boots or shoes. Also, he was without his padded jacket or windbreaker. On his wrist was a watch which had stopped at 5:31.'

Atmanaki:

'The impression was that he tried to go up [the slope], judging by the way his body was situated; and next to his head was a cluster of small saplings in which he was probably stuck. But if he had been heading down, then he would have had to go around them to get into the position where his body was discovered.'

Prosecutor Tempalov's record reads: '[Dyatlov's] left elbow is leaning on a birch sapling, his head is clearly behind the birch and 5-7 cm (1.3-2.3") from it. There are no visible injuries on the body. There is ice on the face and under the chin.'

Radio message sent by the search team: 'We've found the bodies of Dyatlov, Doroshenko, and Krivonischenko or Zolotariov. It is hard to say for sure because there are major injuries on their faces, hands and legs. The prosecutor and Maslennikov are trying to identify them.'

There was one more person present during the search, a journalist named Gennady Grygoryev. Thanks to him, we have more than the official and emotionless reports from the rescue team, and also some verbal inkling of the atmosphere:

We came upon Mount 1079. The weather was calm, and the mountain was as if it was frozen in ice. The snow was compacted. There were ice-covered rock craters all around. The going was so slippery that, as I was carrying the camera and notebook, I almost broke my leg … The corpses were frozen and broken like glass.

Finding the first corpses was devastating for the rescue teams, especially for the students. They came to the site to save their friends, who they believed were only in trouble. They were anxious to find them and bring help. Initially, the students were very eager; they didn't eat and worked up a sweat. Then, once they realised their friends were dead, the tension let up. Silence fell all around.

Atmanaki:

> On completely open, flat snow, swept by wind and snow, Axelrod's dog became interested in something. We dug a little, and under 10 cm (5") of snow we found an elbow. The general location of the body was beneath 50cm (19,5") of snow. The head was pointing in the direction of the tent, and the whole position was typical for a person trying to walk or crawl uphill. The team recognized Kolmogorova.

Prosecutor Tempalov states:

> There are no trees for 70 m (230 ft). The body lies, like the previous bodies, face to the ground on its right side. The arms are bent under the body. Both legs are half bent, and the right is tucked up into her stomach. This gives the impression she was climbing. Her face is covered in blood. In the small of her back there's blood. It can be conjectured that she didn't try to crawl forward, but was trying to maintain her position. There appeared to be no injuries on her body with the exception of some grazes on her face. She probably got these from falling down on the stony ridges.

Radio message sent by the search team:

> We found Kolmogorova with her head fractured – please call for weather information from the 30th of January

to the 2nd of February, because the place and the pose of the bodies suggests a massive wind storm. The prosecutor called for medical experts to see the bodies. The strongest core of the group has been located, which means we must look for the others under the snow. We've found Dyatlov's document bag.

Kolmogorova's body as it was discovered under the snow

In the following days, the search team began checks of the hollow, sweeping the 1500 m (0.930 mi) between the cedar and the tent – 350 m (1148 ft) wide at the top near the tent and narrowing to 200 m (656 ft) wide towards the cedar. The whole brigade performed a methodical search, walking abreast, each forcing probes into the snow at one-metre intervals. In addition to the probes, the area was covered by a thorough free search. Another search was conducted four to five kilometres along the Lozva River. The search produced nothing. No other footprints or animal tracks were found.

Radio message sent by the search team:

3 March – At 6.30 PM the group of Sloptzov and the Mansi, Kourikov, found Dyatlov's depot 400 m (1300 ft) from the rescue camp. In the store were nineteen items of food with a total weight of 55 kg (121 lb). Also found were some medical supplies and Dyatlov's warm outer boots, plus one pair of spare ski boots, a mandolin, a set of batteries and lamps, and an extra set of skis.

The storage depot was found 500 m (0.310 mi) below the top edge of the forest, in the upper reaches of the River Auspiya.

According to guidelines for visitors to the Urals, one person should be allocated 200 grams (0.440 lb) of dried food per person per day. So this amount of food would provide for six or seven days of expedition for the team. There was a full list of food and the note: 'We decided to use the perishable products for our own rescue team.'

The storage depot was constructed well, with fire logs ready for their camp on the way back. The storage dump was located at the spot where the group spent the previous night, and the labaz was well-hidden from view by firewood. Marking it was a pair of skis upright in the snow with a torn gaiter hanging from them.

In the criminal case file, there is another list dated 3 March: 'Things brought from the Storage.' Among them is an ice pick. It isn't clear whether this ice pick was the same one found by the tent or if there was another one in the labaz. If so, this would be strange, considering there was only a single ice pick on the list of items the group stated to have with them. This could, of course, be the same ice pick, but listed along with material from the labaz, since no ice pick was initially reported by those who found the labaz.

*March 5*

As Moses Axelrod recalls, Rustem Slobodin, the strongest member of the group physically, lay face down with arms flung out; on his right hand was a contusion at the base of his thumb. In Axelrod's words:

> One of his legs, the right one I think, was in a valenki, and his left foot, without a valenki, was under his right foot. His face was completely calm without any trace of violence. Under his chest and the rest of the body was a layer of half snow, half ice about 7 cm deep, which gives me reason to think he didn't die immediately but was alive for some time after he lay down. His watch had stopped at 8:45.

The search party students said that while travelling from Sverdlovsk, Rustem Slobodin's father, a university professor, had accompanied them. He was from Ivdel, the closest town to the area of the search, and the place where everyone involved in the search-and-rescue effort had first arrived.

Slobodin's body as it was discovered under the snow

The search team probing the deep snow in the valley of Lozva river

Slobodin Senior was granted permission to come to the camp, and kept asking around if anyone had ever heard of a hunting cabin or cave in the mountains where the rest of the group could have survived. After spending several days at the camp, he went back home without any news regarding Rustem.

The next day, Rustem's body was found.

All the bodies found were transported to Ivdel, where they were examined in the prison hospital's morgue.

Valentin Yakimenko, a member of the search team, shared his memories of that time:

> We lived in a special Army tent and were all together – students and six people in black padded jackets. [The men in black jackets] all had pistols with them and were from a special group of the KGB. There were also about nine invited personnel dressed in white sheepskin bomber jackets with crew cuts, all young.

Every day we worked in deep snow, at least knee deep but often waist deep. So we worked very slowly and for many hours per day, testing with the three-meter probes. Sometimes when our probes touched something and we thought that we had found a body, we would dig feverishly with full power, shovels and hands, but the snow would fall back. Finally, we would find something. 'Oh shit, it's a tree trunk.' We would start again.

Every night, the radio message sent by the search team reported: 'Nothing new. We continue searching.'

The army brought some metal detectors, but they didn't penetrate the snow effectively. In addition, the bodies were half dressed and didn't have significant amounts of metal on them. So the search teams primarily used the three-meter-long metal probes.

The cost of the search operations was very high. There is an official letter from Nicolai Klinov, the Prosecutor of Sverdlovsk region, to S.A. Golunskim, the Director of the National Institution of Research in Criminology, which states:

The enormous expense of the search may keep growing if no new method of searching for the corpses is applied. We know that your institution planned to create a device for spotting bodies buried underground using ultrasound. We heard there were some successful results when the device was used in similar situations. We think it would be reasonable to let us try to use such a device in our current search.

The institute issued an official reply stating that they didn't have a device such as this.

The mood of the camp can be ascertained from Grygoryev's notebook:

All night, yesterday, they spoke about the dead. About why they broke open the tent, etc. It was said that Dyatlov really was full of himself and loved to issue commands. One time he told the group to go from one side of a river to the other for no reason. Simply without reason. One day everyone became so outraged by his behaviour they stopped following his orders. Then he left them and went on a hunger strike.

When he was part of the rank and file he was good. [But as a leader] all mistakes were attributed to him. Two people in particular, who'd been with him before, spoke about this. They said negative things about him as the leader of a group. One said it was stupid for the group to have left at three o'clock, when darkness would fall in one-and-a-half to two hours.

As the search for the remaining members of the group dragged on, some members of the rescue team began to witness strange phenomena. Valentin Yakimenko's diary from March 31:

Today, early in the morning, Victor Mecsheryakov, who was on watch duty, left the tent and saw a light in the sky, like a round sphere. He woke us all. Partly dressed, we left the tent and, for about 20 minutes, we watched the movement of a sphere or round disk until it disappeared behind Mountain 880. We saw it to the southeast of our tent and it was moving in a northerly direction. Before it disappeared, in the very centre of this round sphere, we saw a kind of star, which gradually grew and then started to descend, having detached from the sphere. This occurrence made us really excited and we felt confident it was somehow related to the deaths of the Dyatlov group.

It must be mentioned that on February 17, during the expedition of another group of climbers, something similar was seen. At around 7:30 AM one member of the party on cooking duty called out: 'Come and look, something weird!'

Vladislav Karelin, who joined the rescue team later, subsequently recalled:

> I got out of my sleeping bag without my boots, but in my socks, standing only on branches. I saw a big bright spot. It was growing, and in its centre there was a little star, which also began to grow. This whole spot was moving from the northeast to the southwest and was in the process of falling to the Earth. It left a white tracer tail in the sky. This thing left different impressions on us. Atmanaki said he thought the earth would explode when the object struck, he felt as if it was another planet. As for me, I wasn't really impressed; it was just a falling meteorite. The whole thing took just over a minute.
>
> The snow is melting very fast. To work in this slush is really hard. We've checked the whole slope between the tent and the cedar. It's obvious to us all that we have to search now in the area of the cedar where the depth of the snow can be over three metres.

At that time, they were about to stop the search and postpone the operation until the snow melted, but for some reason they received an order to keep searching.

# 3

The telephone at the university Explorer Club rang constantly. Not just the climbers' parents and relatives, but the general public too, wanted to hear the details. Women university students sat by the telephone every night to take calls. At the same time, even the BBC broadcasted on radio that a group of hikers had been killed near Sverdlovsk.

Yevgeny Zinoviev, the member of Blinov's hiking group whom Lyuda mentioned in her diary, wrote later in his book *Tracks in the Snow*:

> The whole institute, and then the city itself, was buzzing around like a demolished beehive. Everywhere, there were hundreds of questions. 'Where are the young people? What happened to them?' In some circles there were already rumours about atomic tests in the mountains to the north of Ivdel. People living in northern villages had seen the flash, heard the roar, and felt the blow of the shockwave. On top of this, periodically – for example, once every two weeks – strange fireballs were said to appear in the night sky. Starting in January 1959 many people had observed them on the outskirts of Nizhny Tagil, Serov, and Ivdel. The locals were alarmed and rumours were spreading. The authorities were becoming concerned and took measures to bring the situation under control.

As rumour and speculation continued to intensify, the idea that the expedition had been the victim of some kind of mysterious fireball started to gain prominence. Or perhaps the deaths were due to some shady political intrigue? Was that possible?

Vladimir Askinadze, a student and member of the rescue team, states: 'I don't remember who started this, or how it got started, but a rumour began that these students were on a mission to escape from Russia and live abroad. This is precisely what I was told before I left to take part in the search. So, I was called to come to the Party office at the university and they told me [this,] in real seriousness, and that I would need to be attentive, and look out for evidence the group had planned to leave the Soviet Union.'

This time was especially hard for Yuri Yudin, who arrived back at the university after spending the Christmas holidays in his hometown, to hear that his friends were dead. First he was summoned to Ivdel to help catalogue the students' belongings. Then he was summoned to the prison hospital where his friends' bodies were brought. It was then that he identified the bodies of Slobodin and Dyatlov.

He recalls that Slobodin's body had only just been brought to the morgue and was still frozen. To him, the colour of Slobodin's face was like the face of any other living person. Then he was taken to another table, where there was another body covered with a white sheet. He was shown only the face. It was dark and brownish.

'Who is this?' he was asked.

'Igor Dyatlov.'

Then they asked him to go.

Valentina Savina, a nurse who worked at the hospital, recalled that she escorted him out and then saw him 'standing by the wall, crying'.

The relatives of the dead, aside from being distraught, were also under massive pressure from the government. The authorities were unhappy that the entire city of Sverdlovsk was talking about the incident. Yuri Krivonischenko's mother recalls how parents were summoned to Party Committees separately, at different levels of seniority, and were very strongly recommended to bury their children not in Sverdlovsk, but in Ivdel where they were found.

Outraged, the parents insisted on having the funerals at home, and did everything possible to have this matter settled. When the date of the funerals was announced for March 9, and students placed notices about them at the university, they were called to the Community Party office at the university where the local Party chief admonished them loudly and vehemently.

The parents were then informed that on March 9 there would be funerals for only three of the students, and that Yuri Doroshenko and Zina Kolmogorova would be buried at Mikhailovskoe Cemetery, while Yuri Krivonischenko was to be taken to Ivanovskoe Cemetery.

Valentin Yakimenko recalls that Krivonischenko's parents did not mind him being buried at Mikhailovskoe. But instead of Krivonischenko, a student named Nikitin was buried at Mikhailovskoe cemetery. No one knows why.

It was announced that Dyatlov and Slobodin would be buried on March 10, 1959 at Mikhailovskoe Cemetery. Zinoviev reported:

> And here they are, the funerals. In the foyer of the 10th student dormitory on Lenin Street they displayed the decorated coffins of Igor Dyatlov, Zina Kolmogorova, Yuri Doroshenko and Rustem Slobodin. The coffins are open; walking around, everyone has the chance to say goodbye and see first-hand the brown tinged colour and abrasions on the faces of our friends. Bent over them were their parents, relatives and friends with inconsolable tears in their eyes. Relatives of Zina's, who had seen us not long ago in their village, after the December hike [when we] sang nice lyrical

songs with Igor and Zina, of course are now sobbing. It is hard to keep it together; our eyes are full of tears.

Despite, or possibly because of the authorities' strenuous effort to limit interest in the funerals, the number of mourners was enormous. The plan was for the procession to stop for a moment at the university where they had all studied. The police, of course, did not allow this, and the whole crowd was turned away and forced to follow an alternative route. Yuri Kuntsevitch, the head of the Dyatlov Foundation in Yekaterinburg, said:

At that time, I lived next to the cemetery, and was 12 years old, so I was really interested. I tried to push through the crowd to see everything, but it was impossible. I was amazed by some of the people in the crowd. They were wearing trilby style felt hats and had jodhpurs or motorcycle riding pants. They were supervising the procession with their faces blank, expressing nothing. I was standing on a pile of earth at the graveside and I was about eight metres from the bodies. I reckon their skin had a somewhat brick colour, and I spotted some of the students helping to lower the coffins to the graves. It was said they were there despite being forbidden to leave their classes to attend.

There's no one in the world who can identify her child like a mother, yet there were rumours that Doroshenko's body had not been identified by his mother. Was this because she was psychologically unable to look at her dead son with all of his wounds and dark brick skin colour?

Doroshenko's younger sister recalls that they became aware of his death very suddenly. Their family lived very far from Sverdlovsk, in Aktyubinsk, Kazakhstan. Several people in 'dark navy-blue uniforms' came to their house in the middle of the night, and told the mother there had been an accident in the mountains. They took her to fly immediately with them to Sverdlovsk, where she was rushed across town to take part in the funeral ceremony and was only able to see Yuri in his coffin. There are rumours that, for the purpose of the official investigation, Doroshenko was identified by an unnamed girl from the university. Was she the same girl of whom Zina had felt jealous after seeing her holding hands with Yuri? To this day, no one knows. But Zina and her ex-boyfriend were buried side by side, together forever.

The mourners next to Zina Kolmogorova's coffin

# 4

Back on the mountain, in the first days of May, the snow thawed quickly, revealing the ground in shaded areas as well as in the open spaces. Vladimir Askinadze and Boris Suvorov, both UPI students, arrived at the rescue camp. As fate would have it, one of them, Askinadze, would discover the body of Lyuda Dubinina.

But before it happened, there was another remarkable discovery.

According to Askinadze and Suvorov:

> Approximately 50 m (165 ft) down from the cedar on a huge snow drift, Kourikov made out some more small fir tree branches, and noticed these twigs were leading down into the drift. So we began to dig there, and at a depth of 3.5 m (9.8 ft) we found a bed of cut branches. It consisted of 14 firs and one birch, and strewn across the pad were belongings and clothes.

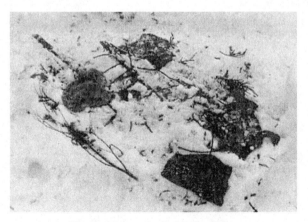

The clothes on a bed of cut branches

The clothes included:

- One leg of a pair of black ski trousers;
- A thick brown woollen sweater;
- A white woollen jumper, made in China; and
- A pair of brown trousers tied at the ankles but flared open with a tear to widen them.

Fifteen metres up the bank from the stream, they found half of a beige sweater as well as the other half of the ski trousers. Fifteen metres from the bower, they found a spoon and a knife sheath.

Pretty soon, about twenty metres from this pad, at a depth of four metres a probe emerged from the snow with a fragment of flesh. They started to dig.

From the official record of the discovery of the bodies:

On the northwest slope of Hill 880, about 50m (164 ft) from the cedar, in the stream, we have discovered four bodies: three men and one woman. The body of the woman has been identified as Lyudmila Dubinina. The bodies of the men cannot be identified without removing them from the water. They are buried in snow 2.5 m (6.5.ft) deep. The men are lying with their heads facing north and downstream, and the body of the woman is lying facing upstream. She is dressed in a small skullcap and a yellow singlet. Then a flannel shirt; two sweaters, one grey the other dark; and on her legs are leggings and brown ski trousers. On one foot are two woollen socks and, on her right foot is bound half of a beige sweater. On the back of her head and on her back there are traces of damage from our probe. Her body is decaying.

The first man is dressed in a khaki-coloured windbreaker, and on his wrist he has two watches, one a Pobeda and the other a Sportif. The Pobeda had stopped at 8:38, and the Sportif showed 8:15. It isn't possible to see the head and legs of this body, because it isn't completely exposed. The other two bodies lie in a kind of hug, both with nothing on their heads, and not all of their hair. They are both dressed in windbreakers, but it is hard to say what else, and it will have to wait until we get them out of the stream. The bodies are decaying and we have photographed them. They need to be taken out of the stream immediately because they are decaying fast and will soon be lost in the stream, which is very fast.

Dubinina's body as it was found in the ravine

It was Vladimir Askinadze's probe that damaged Dubinina's body. Askinadze recently published a letter in *Ural Pathfinder* magazine, in which he recalls that the distance between all the heads of those found in the brook was about 30 cm (11.5") – they were all very close to each other.

Kolevatov body (upper left) was found right next to Zolotariov's as if the latter was carrying or protecting him. Tibo's body was positioned aside of them lower downstream

As for Dubinina, he says her head was laying down on a kind of a natural ledge with water rolling over it. Her mouth was open.

> When we tried to pull them out, we saw Zolotariov had a notebook in one hand and a pen in the other. Ortukov saw this, grabbed the book, read it and immediately cursed Zolotariov with a disparaging word and said: 'He's written nothing.'

Was this really the case, or did he not want others to know what was written in the notebook? George Ortukov was the Army Colonel in charge of logistics and helicopter support. Putting aside for now the possibility of concealment, this is a highly significant comment if it corroborates the timing of the commencement of the disaster. He shouts in disappointment that the last entries in the diary offer no clues and make no mention of problems. It was written in the absence of strangeness or fear.

Askinadze also states that it was hard to identify the bodies as they uncovered them, and it was Ortukov who was saying 'this is x, and here is y'.

'We were surprised,' Askinadze said, 'because it was really hard to see, and no one could object or disagree.'

Askinadze also mentioned that while he was present during that period, he felt very strongly that those in charge were not really interested in a proper investigation. He remembers that the investigator Lev Ivanov 'did not even approach the pad of branches, didn't take pictures, it seemed they already had an explanation.' Askinadze extends this accusation to Ortukov, who was in charge of the whole rescue operation. He wrote: 'If it was really so important to get this right, why didn't they call for Yuri Yudin? He was the only one that knew them all, and could say for sure. I only knew Zina.'

But nothing like this was done, and everything was rushed. This rush was from someone above – from Moscow, Sverdlovsk, or Ivdel. The atmosphere was very tense. Everyone was anxious for answers and waiting for news.

Ortukov and some soldiers took all the bodies from the stream, carried them up the bank and placed them on special stretchers to drag them across the snow, then took them up to the pass and the helicopter pad. It was hard work, and they repeated the same process four times. A helicopter met them on the pass, but the pilots refused to take the bodies on board, complaining this was outside their official duties. It has been said that the pilots knew the bodies were poisoned with radiation and, for this reason, didn't want them in the aircraft.

Ortukov sent a radio message, complaining:

This is a scandal! I and fourteen other people brought these bodies on our shoulders and they refused to take the bodies in spite of me insisting. As a Communist I am outraged by the behaviour of the crew and ask you to inform the Communist Party leader about it. And I have to mention to you for clarity, these bodies are frozen. We packed them for transportation and there was no reason to refuse to take them. The medical expert refused to examine or to cut the bodies here on site. It is absolutely not dangerous from the point of hygiene. They are folded and covered in special impervious material. The crew said they would not transport them until they are in Zinc coffins.

At this time Colonel Ortukov was exhausted and at his limit. He took out his pistol and tried to threaten the crew. Vladimir Askinadze intervened, after which the medical expert reorganized how the bodies should be packed for transportation, and they were finally sent.

# 5

The funerals for the remainder of the group – those found in May – took place on May 12 in Mikhailovskoe Cemetery, except for Zolotariov, who was buried beside Yuri Krivonischenko in Ivanovskoe cemetery.

Zolotariov had no relatives or friends in Sverdlovsk, and it was Sogrin who identified his belongings. Zolotariov's mother was called to come to Sverdlovsk from the Krasnodar area where she lived. She arrived to collect his belongings, as she had been told to, in April, before her son was found. It's known she was not in Sverdlovsk in May when the body was found, and it's likely that the authorities guessed the body was that of Zolotariov, since all the other bodies had already been identified.

This time no one called Yudin to identify the bodies. The secrecy grew tremendously. Only forty years later did Yudin learn of the terrible internal injuries some of his friends had.

These bodies were buried in closed coffins, unlike the ones found in February, which were buried in open coffins as is the usual practice in Russia to this day, except for military deaths. Many years later, in the 1990s, Lev Ivanov, the official investigator for the case, apologized for preventing the parents from dealing with their loved ones in a proper way, not even being allowed to see the faces of their children. But the reasons for his decision are clear enough. In an interview given to a Kazakh newspaper in the 1990s, after his retirement, he said he had made one exception for the father of Lyudmila Dubinina. While she was in the coffin in the morgue, he let her father enter, and permitted someone to open the lid so that he could see her. When he saw his daughter's corpse, he fainted.

Funerals of the last four members of the Dyatlov group

Lyuda's father later wrote to those in charge of the investigation:

> I can't believe this happened in the Soviet Union … the group was badly supplied … no one checked their proposed route… Those heartless leaders were never concerned that, eight days after the planned return date at Vizhay, there was no rendezvous, yet nobody reacted and searches were only initiated on the 21 February.

The emotion in this passage is clear and even as one sympathises with the anguish of a grieving father, one can only imagine the mighty effort it took to pen the word *leaders* instead of *bastards*. Kolevatov's sister Rimma also wrote a letter, full of despair and questions.

I was present at all the funerals of the group. Why were their faces and hands all so dark brown? How can we explain the fact that the four of them who were beside the fire, they were obviously alive, why didn't they try to return to the tent? If they were considerably better dressed, as far as I can see from clothes missing from the tent … if it was a natural disaster, then for sure, after being warmed by the fire, then the guys would have crawled back to the tent. The whole group wouldn't have perished from an Arctic storm!

Testimonies of relatives and eyewitnesses of the funeral, given almost fifty years after the tragedy, mention the dark orange colour of the skin, reminiscent of the colour of bricks. Though unusual, nothing of this was recorded in the official records of the autopsies. At that time, all photography was black and white, so there are no colour pictures of the dead.

In 1962, next to their graves in Mikhailovskoe Cemetery, a monument was erected with pictures of all nine members of the group. Also in 1962, on that pass on Kholat Syakhl mountain, a group led by Valentin Yakimienko set a memorial plaque saying: 'This is the Pass of the Dyatlov Group.'

# PART III:
# THE INVESTIGATION

# 1

The first investigator on the case was Vladimir Korotaev but, as mentioned, he was removed from it after only a few days. He later explained this was due to his refusal to present the cause of death as simple exposure to freezing conditions. In other words, he refused to be party to a cover-up.

However, he said this thirty years after the incident, and there is a certain inconsistency in his words. Korotaev said he was in charge of the investigation 'for only twenty days', but there is information showing that on February 28, two days into the investigation, Lev Ivanov (the only criminal prosecutor in Sverdlovsk in 1959) was already in charge. For example, Lebedev, a member of the rescue team, stated in the criminal case file: 'The next morning (that is, the morning of February 28) in the presence of comrade Ivanov, all of the items were taken out of the tent.'

There is also the supporting statement from Sogrin: 'On the first of March, Axelrod, Tipikin, Lev Ivanov and I were brought by helicopter to the scene.'

It's possible that Korotaev was working for the investigation for less than twenty days, or that he worked at the same time with Ivanov, but not as the investigator; or that the investigation started not on February 26, 1959, when Vasily Tempalov, Ivdel's town prosecutor, launched a formal criminal enquiry.

And there is pretty clear evidence that the investigation started before the official discovery of the first dead bodies. Even though the physical criminal case file was recovered, having suffered from age and frequent use, the initial date of 6 February 1959 was copied without correction on the front cover.

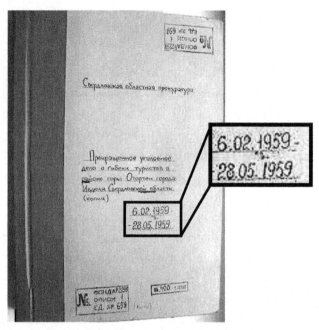

Modern view of the criminal case cover.

In the file there is also a record of an interview with one of the eyewitnesses, Vasily Popov, the head of communications at Vizhai timber department, conducted by the local police chief on February 6, 1959, i.e. twenty days before the official investigation opened!

So it might be that Korotaev was secretly asked to conduct an unofficial investigation before the official one was launched.

We know that Korotaev was working with the Mansi and hurricane theories. Thirty-seven years after the incident, he mentioned in a speech that the Mansi were under the heavy suspicion, but they pointed to the wind as a possible cause of the deaths of the Dyatlov group, saying that the wind can be so strong it carries people away.

At that point the bodies had yet to be examined, and Korotaev gives the following reason for releasing the Mansi:

> When the tent was brought to my office for investigation, a woman entered the room and, when she saw the tent, she said she had worked for 30 years as a seamstress in *Ivdelag* (prison); and she took one look at the fabric of the tent and told me the tent was cut from the inside, not the outside. For me, this was significant, and I ordered the tent to be sent for a forensic examination.

The examination proved that the tent was cut from inside; this was the formal reason for clearing the Mansi of suspicion. There were other reasons for doing so:

1. The Mansi were friendly to Russians.
2. Had the Mansi done it, they might have been expected to have taken alcohol from the tent because of their love of drinking.
3. The area was not sacred for them so they had no motivation to kill there.

Soon after releasing the Mansi, Korotaev refused to continue investigation according to instructions, and he was fired. Lev Ivanov, who was assigned to the case after him, managed to complete the entire investigation in only three months. He demonstrated a concerted effort to analyse what was known and an obvious desire to uncover the truth.

The criminal case file opens with two typed copies of each of the diaries found. These include the group's general diary and the diary of someone else, wrongly attributed to Zina Kolmogorova. Zina's real diary is available at the Dyatlov Foundation, but the copy presented in the criminal case is completely different.

The diaries are followed by an interesting document, which is also a typewritten copy, this time of an ersatz newspaper called the *Otorten Evening News*. There is evidence that this spoof newspaper, found in the group's tent, had been created by the hikers themselves for fun.

It's believed that the student's humorous news sheet was pinned to the inside of the tent, but none of the rescue party reported seeing it. However, Moses Axelrod, who shared a tent with Ivanov, later wrote in his memoirs that Ivanov showed the original to him.

The tradition of creating this kind of 'newspaper' was typical of that time. In every school and institution, the students regularly made posters with headings, articles and drawings. The point was to present news, or a social problem, in a satirical way, and was a popular method to gently hint at some criticism, or to bring something of interest to light.

What is certain is that a copy of something was included in the papers for the criminal prosecution. It isn't known who made the copy, and the original appears to have vanished, but the circumstantial evidence is that the original document is indeed a spoof newspaper that Dyatlov and his team made, not long before the Dyatlov Pass incident occurred.

From the *Otorten Evening News*, Issue 1, 1 February 1959:

### SCIENCE
Lately in scientific circles there has been a very lively debate about the existence of Yeti. According to the latest data, the snowmen live in the northern Urals, in the area of the Otorten Mountain.

### PHILOSOPHY
Ski hikers and love. Philosophical seminar every day in the tent main building, and these lectures will be given by Dr Tibeaux Ph.D., and Dubinina (MA in love science).

### TECHNICAL NEWS
Hiking sledge – very good for riding in trains, in the car, and on a horse. But not really any good for transportation of loads over the snow. For further information please turn to the main constructor Kolevatov.

Fun puzzles. Is it possible to warm nine ski hikers with one blanket?

### SPORTS
The team of radio experts, consisting of Doroshenko and Kolmogorova, set a new world record in contesting how fast they could put together pieces of the stove. The record is one hour, two minutes, and 27 seconds.

The spoof newspaper is significant in that it is almost certainly the very last thing the group members wrote before their deaths. Also, the creation of the *Otorten Evening News* suggests there was a normal atmosphere in the group, where they could tease each other without danger of being misunderstood. Also it speaks for the fact that it was not too cold inside the tent, and the weather conditions outside were not too harsh.

In the criminal case folder, the witness statements are found immediately after the spoof newspaper:

Ivan Rempel, forester of the Vizhay Region:

On January 25 a group of hikers came to me and showed me their route, asking what would be the best route to the summit of Mount Otorten, and they also asked me if they could see my own map of the area. While I was looking over their route I told them it is dangerous to go on the Urals ridge in winter, because there are deep crevasses and some holes where one can fall. Anyway, the winds there are so severe they can actually blow people down.

But they just told me this kind of expedition would be graded at the highest level of difficulty. I told them to go ahead. I showed them my map, they checked it against their own route map, and noted some edges and boundaries of the woods in that area. I advised them to take a closer route along one of our forest rides. They told me they would decide when they reached the Second Severniy mining camp.

I think they could only have died from a natural disaster and climate conditions. I don't think the Mansi would have hurt them. I meet [Mansi] all the time and they are always friendly and hospitable. From what old people have told me, there have been a number of people that perished while trying to cross the Ural ridge before. Mansi live in the area, but they don't have their sacred stones or secret places in that spot.

Vasily Popov, a local inhabitant, said he 'saw two groups of hikers in the first days of February, and at that time the wind was bringing so much snow the drifting was severe. I have lived in the settlement of Vizhay since 1951, and I cannot remember any winds as bad as this.'

Then there is Ivan Pashin's testimony. Pashin was one of the local guides, who was escorting Slobtsov and Sharavin when they discovered the tent. He refused to approach it. He officially testified:

At the approximate time when these hikers died, even in our settlement of Vizhay, the winds were so extreme they made children fall. I've been a hunter here since my early years and I can remember people dying in these kinds of winds. Sometimes we've waited six days without food, trapped in the shelter of a ravine waiting for the wind to stop. When the Mansi came to our area to search, they acted very naturally. It was obvious they felt sorry for those students and they tried to help.

Nearly all of the locals state the same thing: the winds were severe and the Mansi wouldn't have hurt Dyatlov's group. The records for the investigation of the Mansi themselves are short and uninformative, given that most of them were questioned via an interpreter. The further records of the interviews with local sports and University officials are not of particular interest, since they are only standard questions and answers of those who simply wanted to prove they were not responsible for what happened.

The case file also contains the weather report for February 1 for the Ivdel region. It reads: 'The wind was north-northwest at 1-3 m/s. No snowstorms, windstorms, nor blizzards were observed.'

The wind speed mentioned is equal to 3.73 – 6.84 mph, which is a 'light breeze' according to the Beaufort scale. However, since Ivdel is 72 miles south of the place of the tragedy it is worth comparing data from other weather stations in the area. This comparison gives us an average figure of approximately 12.43 mph (5,5 m/s) or a 'moderate breeze' according to the Beaufort scale.

A radio message sent by the search team to the headquarters of the operation stated:

> We found four different people in four different places, all underdressed and without footwear, which gives us reason to guess they were blown out of their tent during a blizzard. A severe blizzard threw the victims away from the tent without *valenki*, and some without trousers or jackets. The direction of the windstorm was northeast. That's why all of them were found in one line from the tent, and the most remote was found almost two km from the tent.

At the same time the members of the search-and-rescue team, expedition-savvy as they were, doubted that the group would undress in the tent. Grygoryev expresses their shared opinion in his notes:

It's unusual to undress completely in the tent. As for those who are dressed, this doesn't suggest duties as night guards. There's no such thing as a night guard. If someone was on guard duty, then the next day would be difficult and they would fall behind everyone else.

A radio reply sent to the search team asked why the tent and belongings remained if the people had been blown away from the tent.

Grygoryev's notebook reads: 'The tent had been set up well. From the side of the summit they dug it into the snow, and the snow came from that side. So, the wind only whisked over the roof.'

In his testimony for the criminal case, Captain Chernyshov stated: 'It might be that the wind urged the people apart, but it did not actually drag them across the snow or there could have been no prints at all.'

Vadim Brusnitsin, a member of the search party, was on the pass and experienced the power of the wind himself. He told the investigators the wind could not have carried the members of the Dyatlov group away from the tent. 'Even at the tent site itself where the steepness of the slope reached 20 degrees, enough to lie in the direction of the wind, you would have stayed in place,' he said.

Indeed, when Rustem Slobodin's body was found, Moses Axelrod noticed that 'on his head a small cap was perched insecurely. This was strange because if there had been any wind it would have been lost.'

Moreover, the windstorm did not explain why the tent had cuts in it.

Here are the results of the examination of the tent, filed in the criminal case:

It has been established that on the surface of the tent there are some damaged areas, caused as the result of an impact by some sharp weapon such as a knife, as well as some tears. The first piece of damage looks like a jagged line, 32 cm (12") in length. Above is a small piercing of the fabric, about 2.2 cm (0.7") long, and the corners of the piercing are slightly torn. The second and third damage points have a somewhat irregularly curved shape. Their approximate lengths are 89 cm (35") and 42 cm (16"). From both sides of the third cut, pieces of fabric are missing – it's just a hole. Next to the cut edges, there is some superficial damage to the fabric that looks like insignificant tears and abrasions. All of them are rectilinear in shape. The character and the shape of all the above mentioned damage are evidence that they were formed because of action on the fabric from the inside with the blade of some tool.

The tent as it was examined during the investigation. Photo from the criminal case files

The records show that many members of the rescue team were questioned about windstorms and other possible factors, such as the presence of unknown parties on the slope. Some of their testimonies have already appeared in the description of the rescue operation, and others will be quoted later.

Around the time of these inquires Ivanov began to create his version of events, which was murder. But just as had been the case with Korotaev, he became closely supervised. He was called to Moscow and, according to the testimony of members of the search party, came back a different man.

After this, the nature of the investigation changed. Not only did it become more covert, but it was also apparent that the investigators were much less active – merely 'going through the motions' – and no longer interested in uncovering the truth.

But deep inside himself, Lev Ivanov, as he stated many years later, was extremely eager to understand what had happened. Could it, he wondered, have been a murder by escaped or former inmates of the Ivdelag prisons? The whole area of the northern Urals was full of gulags, and Ivdel alone had four such institutions. Sites in the forest were reserved for those with life sentences, and there were seven prison camps within Ivdelag. So Ivanov decided to check if there were any reports of escaped prisoners. There were none. In addition, the following facts contradicted the theory of an escaped prisoner murdering the group:

1. No money was taken (and they were carrying quite a lot), nor valuable equipment or survival kits, not even a bottle of spirits. Nothing of this nature was missing.

2. The prisoners would perhaps not have let the girls go. The examination of the bodies later revealed that both girls died as virgins.

3. In winter in Russia, prisoners normally have more sense than to try breaking out of prison. In the taiga, they simply cannot survive without food, skis, and a tent, and the distance from Dyatlov Pass to the camps is almost 100 km.

But what if the students killed each other as a result of a terrible conflict or due to the effects of alcohol?

Ivanov didn't believe in such a scenario. Because conditions during a mountain expedition are so demanding, such tours tend to cause the participants to reveal their individual personalities. Once someone has proved to be unreliable or not suited to the demands or culture of the rest of the group, he or she has little chance of being invited on subsequent expeditions.

Most of the group had already gone to the mountains several times together. As one reads their diaries, especially in the original Russian, it becomes obvious that even if they had some disagreements, such as who had to sleep next to the furnace or sew the tent, those disagreements were not about serious matters and didn't cause tension in the group. An example is the passage in Lyuda's diary, where she writes that Krivonischenko 'moved to the second part of the tent while cursing terribly and accusing us of betrayal.'

For a Russian reader this, 'cursing terribly' is nothing but a half-joking expression, a piece of hyperbole used as a figure of speech.

Their pictures reveal the atmosphere of adventure and fun. Ivanov had all the film from the group's cameras developed in the University's laboratory.

He asked student Boris Bychkov and his friends to print as many pictures as they could and distribute them amongst friends, students and relatives. When asked why, Ivanov said: 'Some people want to present this tragedy as a result of the conflict amongst the group. Let them see these pictures and realise that couldn't have happened!'

Dubinina and Krivonishenko (left), Tibo (laughing) and Slobidin

It has been suggested that, as a result of a conflict, someone jumped out of the tent and the rest of the group chased after him or her to catch up with them and bring them back. In any conflict in a group of this size and composition, there are always people who remain neutral. In the event of a conflict, someone would have stayed in the tent. And certainly at least one person would have stayed alive as there was food, clothing, skis, fire, etc.

Ivanov also talked to Yudin who confirmed that 'there were not any particular dislikes among the group'. And with regards to personal feelings, 'it was just like any mixed company.'

The only new participant in the expedition was Zolotariov, but he quickly became very popular. Yudin testified that, 'Zolotariov was widely accepted. He was a walking encyclopaedia of songs; everyone copied songs from him.' Judging by the photos, Zolotariov and Tibo got on very well, and would often ski in close proximity.

Tibo (left) and Zolotariov

As someone who had been through the war, Zolotariov knew hardship and understood what it meant to be mutually supportive. It's theoretically possible, with Dyatlov's authoritarian leadership and Zolotariov's background and life experience, that different points of view could have arisen regarding expedition decisions.

Even though it has been the subject of conjecture, there is no evidence in the diaries that Zolotariov ever tried to seize leadership of the group.

Ivanov still believed in the murder theory but rejected the self-destruction theory. The findings in May greatly complicated his task because the injuries of the bodies were very hard to explain. They probably were not caused by human beings at all...

# 2

The autopsy reports make the most painful reading in the evidence for the criminal case. Not every picture of the dead bodies in the morgue was included in the case files. In 2009, Lev Ivanov's daughter gave some to the Dyatlov Foundation. Most of them are available on the Internet now.

The post mortem on the first five bodies determined that the cause of death was freezing. The first five bodies were Doroshenko, Krivonischenko, Zina, Dyatlov and Slobodin. Their injuries were not life-threatening and it was concluded that they died from freezing, not from being injured. Slobodin, however, had suffered a major head trauma. He had a fracture from the left temporal bone along the direction of the upper forward area of the lobular bone with a dehiscence of 0.1 cm and a length of 6 cm. It was not possible to determine whether it was a result of a blow or due to the freezing process (when a brain freezes its volume increases, and if there is a small fracture already in the skull, it can be expanded).

The last four, Dubinina, Zolotariov, Tibeaux and Kolevatov had no visible injuries on their bodies, but when the dissections were conducted in the morgue in Sverdlovsk, it was found that three of them had considerable injuries to their internal organs. For instance, four of Lyuda Dubinina's ribs were broken on the right, and six were broken on the left. One part of a broken rib had even penetrated her heart. Tibo's skull was fractured, but in a very strange way: without bruising.

On May 28, 1959, the Junior Counsellor of Justice and Criminal Prosecutor of Sverdlovsk region, Lev Ivanov, led the interrogation of an expert with the observance of Article 169-173 of the Criminal Procedural Code of the RSFSR.

The expert gave the following information about himself:

1. Last name, first name, patronymic: Vozrozhdenny Boris Alekseevich.
2. Year of birth: 1922.
3. Place of birth: Gomel, BSSR.
4. Education:
   a. Show when and where you graduated from school: Graduated in 1954 from the Sverdlovsk State Medical Institute.
   b. Show when and where you received your special training or production skills in your specialty: In the department of forensic pathology.
   c. Have you received any awards for any work, writings, or inventions in your field? No.
5. Experience in your field: Doctor since 1954.
6. Currently employed as: A forensic pathologist.
7. Party affiliation (if a member of the CPSU, show rank): No party.
8. Prior criminal convictions: None.
9. Permanent address (exact address and telephone number): Kollektivnaya St. 5, apt 15, Sverdlovsk.

Question: From what kind of force could Tibo have received such damage?

Answer: In the conclusion, it's shown the damage to Tibo's head could have been the result of the throwing, fall or jettisoning of the body. I don't believe these wounds could have been the result of Tibo simply falling from the level of his own height, i.e. falling and hitting his head. The extensive, depressed, multi-splintered (broken fornix and base of the skull) fracture could be the result of an impact of an automobile moving at high speed. This kind of trauma could have occurred if Tibo had been thrown and fallen and hit his head against rocks, ice, etc., by a gust of strong wind.

Question: Is it possible that Tibo was hit by a rock that was in someone's hands?

Answer: In this case, there would have been damage to the soft tissue, and this was not evident.

Question: How long could Tibo have lived after the trauma. Could he have moved on his own, talked, etc.?

Answer: After this trauma, Tibo would have had a severe concussion; that is, he would have been in an unconscious state. Moving him would have been difficult and, close to the end, movement would not have been possible. I believe he would not have been able to move even if he had been helped. He could only have been carried or dragged. He could have shown signs of life for 2-3 hours.

Question: How is it possible to explain the cause of the damage to Dubinina and Zolotariov? Is it possible to combine them into one cause?

Answer: I think the character of the wounds on Dubinina and Zolotariov – a multi-splintered fracture of the ribs – on Dubinina were bilateral and symmetrical, and on Zolotariov were one-sided. Both had haemorrhaging into the cardiac muscle with haemorrhaging into the pleural cavity, which is evidence of them being alive [when injured] and is the result of the action of a large force, similar to the example used for Tibo. These wounds, especially appearing in such a way without any damage to the soft tissue of the chest, are very similar to the type of trauma that results from the shock wave of a bomb.

Question: How long could Dubinina and Zolotariov have lived?

Answer: Dubinina died 10-20 minutes after the trauma. She could have been conscious. Sometimes it happens that a person with a wound to the heart (for example, a serious knife wound) can talk, run and ask for help. Dubinina's situation was one of complicated traumatic shock resulting from the bilateral rib fracture, with subsequent internal haemorrhaging into the pleural cavity. Zolotariov could have lived longer. It needs to be taken into account that they were all trained, physically fit, and hardened people.


It was after this report that Ivanov started considering the 'overwhelming force,' and in his opinion, it came from above.

Some parts of the criminal case files are devoted to a phenomenon dubbed the 'fireballs in the sky.' For some reason, Lev Ivanov included this data, and later it becomes more obvious why he was interested in these testimonies. The meteorologist, Tokareva, gives the most detailed description of the fireball:

To the Director of the Ivdel Police Department 15.03.59: At 6:50 AM local time a comet was seen in the sky. The tail was similar to that of dense cirrus clouds. Then the star became free from the tail, became brighter, and flew away. It began gradually to swell and became a large ball surrounded in mist. Inside this ball a star began to burn, from which, first, a crescent was formed, and then an entire ball, but not as bright. The large ball began to fade and became like a blur. It disappeared at 7:05 AM. The star moved from the south to the northeast.

Atmanaki:

On the 7th of February, Vladimir Shevkunov and I got up at 6 AM to cook breakfast for the rest of the rescue group. It was grey and I saw a kind of milk white spot, approximately five or six times the diameter of the moon, consisting of five or six concentric circles. It reminded me of a kind of lunar halo. I told my colleague that the moon looked weird, and he replied: 'That's not the moon,' and 'It's supposed to be in a different part of the sky.'

At that moment, in the very centre of the white spot, a star sparkled, and then the star began to grow and move fast in a westerly direction. In several seconds, it grew to the size of the moon and then it broke out of the cloud and appeared as a huge fiery white disk about the size of two moons. And it was still surrounded by the pale white rings.

Staying the same size, the sphere began to fade until it became the same as the whole aureola, and then the whole thing just dissolved in the sky.

The whole thing took no more than about one-and-a-half minutes and was really strange. I got the impression it was some kind of cosmic body falling down, but then when it was growing the thought came to my mind that our earth was about to collide with another planet and maybe be destroyed.

During all this time we were standing as if we were hypnotised watching all this. I spoke to many people about it, those who had also seen it, and people who were in their houses say the light was so bright that it woke them.

The file contains an excerpt from the local newspaper with a story, which was indeed strange, as in the Soviet era everything was strictly secular and could be explained by science.

On February 7, 1959 the *Tagil Worker* reported:

Yesterday at 6:55 AM local time, to the south-east, at an angle of twenty degrees above the horizon, a bright globe appeared, about moon sized. Around 7 AM, inside of this globe, there was some sort of explosion and a very bright core of this globe became visible, which started to glow more intensely, and around it appeared a cloud. Then the cloud dissolved in the whole eastern part of the sky. Soon after this a second explosion took place, and it resembled the crescent of the moon, gradually the cloud was glowing and in the centre of it remained the bright spot.

– A. Kissel, Deputy Head of Vysokogorny Colliery.

A radio message was sent by the search team from the rescue group on March 31, 4:00 AM:

In the southeast direction the soldier on duty, Misherakov, noticed a large fiery ring, which was moving away from us for about 20 minutes, and then it disappeared behind Mount 880. Before it vanished below the horizon, from the centre of the ring a star appeared, and this star grew to about the size of the moon and then detached from the ring and began to fall. All personnel that were awake observed this strange phenomenon. Please, we ask you to explain this to us, and how safe should we feel, because it made a pretty alarming impression.

– Avenbourg, Sogrin and Potapov

Under the orders of Investigator Ivanov, an examination was made of the clothes of some expedition members, in order to determine if there was any radioactive contamination on the clothes or the dead bodies.

To order a radiological examination was by no means a regular part of the investigative process. The examination was conducted on May 18, in a poorly equipped city laboratory, almost ten days after the last funeral. Vladimir Levashov, the main radiologist of Yekaterinburg, conducted the examination. Levashov's report reads: 'The absence of adequate equipment and the conditions in our laboratory did not allow us to conduct radiochemical and spectrometric analysis for defining the chemical structure of the emitter and measuring the energy of its emission.'

It's possible that in May, Ivanov received some information or an order to conduct this examination. It's also possible this was done on his own initiative. If it had been ordered from above, the examination would have taken place in the best possible laboratory, which, at that time in the USSR, would have been in a military institution. As it was, Ivanov contacted the rescue party member Albert Kikoin whose brother, Isaak Kikoin, was in charge of a national laboratory for studying radiation.

Levashov was warned that this investigation was to be a matter of secrecy and he signed a document to confirm he wouldn't release the information to anyone but the investigator. He was provided with all the clothes of Zolotariov, Dubinina, Kolevatov, and Tibeaux, as well as bio-culture samples of their bodies.

The four subjects of the examination were given numbers:

No. 1: Kolevatov
No. 2: Zolotariov
No. 3: Tibeaux
No. 4: Dubinina

The results of the radiological investigation, recorded in the criminal case report, were as follows:

Clothes examined:
- Brown sweater taken from body No. 4: 9900 decay per minute from 150 square centimetres.
- Lowest part of the long johns: 5000 decay per minute from 150 square centimetres.
- Part of the sweater from body No. 1: 5600 decay per minute from 150 square centimetres.

Upon rinsing the clothes, it was shown that contamination could be decreased by between thirty and sixty percent. The rinse was conducted in a standard test using cold running water for three hours.

Conclusions:
1. The materials examined contained radioactive traces within normal limits of the natural content for the potassium 40 isotope.

2. Examined separately, samples of the clothes contained several higher than normal quantities of radioactive compounds that are beta emitters.

3. It was confirmed, from tests involving rinsing with water, that the radioactive substances found displayed a tendency to be reduced by such a test. Thus their presence proves that they were not caused by a neutron stream or by the incidence of induced radioactivity, but by the contamination of radioactive beta particles.

Additional questions the investigator asked Levashov were as follows:

Question: Could the clothes be contaminated above the normal level by normal circumstances without having been in the presence of a radioactive-contaminated place?

Answer: No

Question: Were the samples examined by you contaminated?

Answer: As mentioned in the conclusion, there is contamination by a radioactive substance or substances. Beta emitters were found on certain separately-sampled areas from the samples I received. For example, the sample from body no. 4 (brown sweater), at the moment of examination, had a decay rate of 9900 beta particles per minute for 150 square centimetres. After rinsing, it displayed 5200 decays of beta particles per minute from 150 sq cm.

Normally, contamination of beta particles from 150 sq cm should not exceed 5000 before rinsing. After rinsing it would be expected to find a normal level equivalent to the natural base level, which is provided by natural cosmic radiation for all people in a particular place. This is the normal rule for those who work with radioactive materials. From body No. 1, the sweater yielded a display of 5600 particles per minute before rinsing, falling to 2700 particles per minute after rinsing. In your data it's indicated that, before they were sent to us, all of these objects had been in running water for quite some time, which means they had already been rinsed.

Question: Can we conclude that the clothes were contaminated by radioactive dust?

Answer: Yes. Contaminated by radioactive dust which fell down from the atmosphere, or these clothes were contaminated while working with radioactive substances, or via contact. This particular contamination exceeds the normal level for people who work with radioactive substances.

Question: What was the real degree of contamination of some objects considering that they were in running water for about 15 days?

Answer: One can guess the contamination of some parts of the clothes was many times more. But we must also consider that the clothes could have been washed with differing degrees of intensity.

May 29, 1959

On May 28, 1959, soon after the radiological experiment was conducted, the criminal case was closed, as it was clear there would be no perpetrators to prosecute. The official statement giving the reason for closing the case also amounted to a de facto conclusion of what was believed officially to have happened. This statement was written by Lev Ivanov:

> The deaths of the expedition members were due to a series of mistakes by Dyatlov. On 1 February he began the ascent to the summit at three PM, even though he knew about the difficulty of the terrain.
>
> Furthermore – and this was Dyatlov's next mistake – he chose a line 500 m (1640 ft) to the left of the planned pass that lies between Summit 1079 and Summit 880. So the group found themselves on the eastern slope of Summit 1079. They used what was left of the daylight to ascend to the summit in strong winds (which are typical for this area) and low temperatures of minus 25 C ( - 10 F). Dyatlov found himself in bad conditions for the night, so he decided to pitch his tent on the slope of 1079 so as to start in the morning without adding the distance from the forest (~1 km/ 0.6 mi) to the remaining trek of about 10 km (6.2 mi) to the summit.
>
> Considering the absence of external injuries to the bodies or signs of a fight, as well as the abandonment of all the valuable kit, plus the conclusions of the medical examinations for the causes of the deaths, it has to be concluded that the cause of their deaths was calamity or overwhelming force.

From 1959 onwards, this file was kept in the archives of the prosecutor's office. In March 1989, the first photocopies of the criminal case were made. There were rumours that five pages were missing from the original file, but this was not confirmed.

# PART IV: THE MYSTERY DEEPENS

# 1

The enigmatic story of the Dyatlov group's last trip is something like Alice's journey down the rabbit hole. But unlike Alice's trip into Wonderland, the journey isn't over yet, and indeed may never be, for the ultimate truth of what happened to Dyatlov and his friends will probably never be known. All that's certain is that the group died in an unpleasant, mysterious way.

Keeping in mind the principle of Occam's razor – which, in a very elementary interpretation, means that the simpler hypothesis is is generally the most accurate one – it's logical to begin with the most logical explanations.

The explanation of an avalanche could answer many questions, but it's hard to imagine an avalanche on such a low-angled slope (of only 15 degrees). Still, it might have occurred all the same. But in fact the possibility of an avalanche was not even discussed by the people on Mount 1079 in 1959, even though the most popular subject for discussion was what made the group flee from their tent.

Inquisitive forensic minds today have proposed that it was not an avalanche in the classical sense of the word, but a 'snow slab', the convergence of different layers of snow a few metres below the surface. To set up a tent it is necessary first to flatten the ground beneath it, and the members of the Dyatlov group, in doing this, may have carelessly broken through the layers of snow. The tent was sufficiently large for this to have happened, and so the area cleared was also large – at least two square metres.

The hypothesis here is that, in removing the excess snow, the Dyatlov group removed the support of the overlying layers, resulting in a shift of the snow slabs. This shift resulted in the partial filling of the tent with snow, on top of the people sleeping inside. The snow, which would have been hardened under its own weight, could even have caused injuries.

The cuts on the tent could be explained by the possibility that, to stay alive, the expedition members first cut small holes so as to determine the depth of the snow that was covering them and to allow air to enter the tent, and then made longer cuts so they could escape from the tent.

The hypothesis goes on to suggest that the wounded were taken out of the tent, and removed to the shelter of the trees where they were laid on the ground, and then the others decided to return to the tent to gather the remaining items for warmth. They would have made the fire, but couldn't stay warm enough, and froze to death.

This version is plausible, but there's a range of arguments against it.

First of all, there were well-trained experts who saw the scene and the slope immediately after the tent was found. One of these was the alpinist Abram Kikoin who, during the Second World War, was an instructor for ski-mounted troops in the Gorelnik mountain camp below Alma-Ata, where close attention was paid not only to the technical preparation of trainees, but also to avalanche safety in the mountains.

There were also Maslennikov, Sogrin, Axelrod and other hikers with very extensive experience. Sogrin had been a pathfinder since he was in school, and by 1959 he had fulfilled all of the requirements to become a mountain leader. In that role, his main expeditions had been in the northern and sub-arctic regions of the

Urals, as well as climbing the Narodnaya (mountain of People), Sablya (Sword), and Neroika mountains.

In general, the northern Urals are not considered to be a zone of 'potential avalanche danger' (indicating no previous history of avalanches in that area), which is not the case with the sub-arctic Urals, where avalanches have frequently occurred, and so might be expected to occur again.

Sogrin stated the following in his article published in the *Ural Pathfinder* in November 2010:

> From personal experience of being on different mountains of the northern Urals in winter, and not even considering the long time spent in the search area, I have never experienced, nor seen evidence of, avalanches or [the] danger of an avalanche [there]. In the 1950s many groups of hikers from Sverdlovsk trekked through the northern Urals. And no one ever warned [them] about the danger of avalanches along these paths. It could be argued that avalanches don't happen in the forest zone, but higher on the bare mountains.

On the other hand, looking hard at the search area, it's clear that all the peaks are slightly raised above a dividing ridge and have very gentle slopes. This watershed itself is a plateau. Such a relief pattern is characteristic of the northern Urals, with the only exception being, perhaps, the Denezhkin Kamen, which is located on the side away from the dividing ridge. The snow on these slopes and plateaus is so blown by the wind that the slope is almost completely free of snow, which only fills up uneven areas. The lion's share of the snow is simply whirled into the valleys (where there is indeed a lot of it). Consequently, on Otorten it is often actually easier to climb without snowshoes or skis.

When the area around the tent was carefully examined in 1959, considerable attention was paid to the fact that, higher up, the slope flattens out and turns into a horizontal dividing line almost devoid of snow and absent of any avalanche catchment (a place where snow accumulates, ready to collapse into an avalanche under favourable conditions). So, where would an avalanche have come from?

A Russian avalanche specialist, K. Losev, expressed the fear that if the forest on the slopes was felled there could be a full-fledged avalanche. This happened on the slopes of *Khibin*, on the Kola Peninsula, where there is an absence of vegetation. Avalanches are common there, and the mechanism of their formation is associated with snow storms and strong winds that carry the snow from the bare mountains into the valleys.

During the search party's investigations, it was clear that the snow on the tent was accumulated by the wind. If there had indeed been a layer of snow (a snow slab) on the tent, then it wouldn't have been difficult to differentiate it from the rest of the snow. A snow slab has a completely different structure and density. It would have needed more than skis to destroy it by digging; an axe and good steel shovel would have been required, and it would take a good deal of strength. In addition, the remains of a snow slab typically persist until summer, and are difficult to melt. That was not the case here.

Sogrin explains that, during the breakage of a snow slab, the whole slope below the line of separation moves (it no longer holds on to anything), and the underlying layer from the deep hoarfrost acts like ball bearings on which the layers of snow rush downwards. If this type of avalanche hits a person, it can result in serious traumatic injuries.

Sogrin states:

I happened to be a witness to this kind of avalanche. During a winter expedition to Tien Shan on a path that was the third degree of difficulty, our group had to traverse a slope with a height of somewhere up to 300 metres. It was January. When we stepped onto the slope, we understood that under us was a ripe snow slab. It was only necessary to provide an impulse, and the whole slope would be set in motion. Rising above the slope, we headed in the right direction.

When we had travelled about half of the distance we were planning to travel, we heard a small click and a crack formed along our tracks and further over the whole slope. The snow slab settled from the load (we had five people with us with heavy backpacks). We didn't have time to come to our senses, as the whole underlying slope of hundreds of square metres cracked up on huge boulders and slid downwards. We stayed on the loose, deep hoarfrost, and in front of us a vertical [of] up to 1-1.5 m ( 3.2 ft) rose up, the wall from the line [where] the avalanche [broke] with the above slope, which wasn't dangerous for us anymore, as it had already been taken, and snow slabs don't move more than once. We finished the traverse moving along loose snow.

Knowing all of these processes going on in the winter snow cover, I studied very closely the state of the snow around the tent of the Dyatlov group. There were no signs of the occurrence of deep hoarfrost. If it had occurred (and this is crystalline ice), then it wouldn't have gone anywhere until the spring melting.

The columns of compressed snow from the tracks of the group going from the tent could not have become a snow slab (it's too dense) or hoarfrost (it is granular, like sugar).

This was also the opinion of other experts. It was only later that Axelrod tried to use the avalanche idea to explain things. Askinadze, the man who found Dubinina's body, asked him: 'Could you be scared into such behaviour by an avalanche?' He wouldn't reply.

Sogrin continues:

To be consistent, the whole slope from the tent to the *Lozva* valley, becoming steeper, should also have been an area of avalanche danger with the development of hoarfrost and snow slabs. However, from the end of February to May the search parties not only didn't trigger an avalanche, but didn't even see the possibility of one developing.

Believe me, we walked along the whole valley from the tent to the woods, around 1.5 km (0.6 mi). Our feet covered every inch of ground. The snow was not deep: some places sufficiently solid, other places we sank up to our knees, and closer to the cedar it was a little deeper. There wasn't even a small sliding of snow from our actions.

Some of the rescue party saw skinned bark on some of the trees, but this pattern was [found even] on [other] parts of the terrain. Blizzards create snow drifts, from stinging snow like a polishing stone, changing the external appearance of plants. These [apparent] traces of avalanches are visible everywhere from the prevailing westerly winds, regardless of the orientation of the slopes of the terrain. All the limbs of the trees can be oriented with the wind, to the east like a flag; an avalanche has nothing to do with this.

There are variations of this avalanche theory: it has been speculated that the tent was simply set up in a poorly chosen area and, while they were trying to erect it, the Dyatlov group dug the snow away from above the tent, and this removed the support for an overhanging mass of snow. At first they didn't realise what had happened, some were injured, and the group panicked and rushed away downhill. Once they were in the ravine they tried to build a snow hole for shelter and it happened again.

While the bodies were in the brook, the clothes could have picked up some lightly radioactive mud from the brook and ground. The explanation for why the tongues and the eyes were missing from some of the corpses was because of the action of the water and of animal scavengers such as birds, mice and other small rodents.

Sogrin states:

I can suggest that, after setting up the tent, as a result of its being based below the surface of the snow, the upper level of the snow could have collapsed for some reason onto the side of the tent or have plastered over it under the action of the wind. In my experience this has happened many times when camping and on expeditions into the mountains. This happens because of wind, snowfall and 'streams' of snow running down a slope.

In central Tien Shan, we were in an avalanche of freshly fallen wet snow. For us, the victims, we set up a tent on a ledge under a rock. After some time, a small 'avalanche' fell on us, which began to fill the area between the cliff and the side of the tent, pushing us further and further from the rock. The snow fell on our backs and shoulders, and we tried to resist the force of this load. However, even then, as in other cases, the thought never arose to abandon the tent and flee.

What is more, Dyatlov most likely wouldn't have ended up in this situation anyway, as he knew the tent was set up in a completely safe area, and snow was collapsing the tent flaps (this happened earlier), which creates a certain inconvenience, but is not catastrophic.

In addition, Sogrin is sure that Dyatlov knew a snow slab doesn't happen twice; therefore, the students wouldn't have been so afraid of a repeat movement of the snow to have run 100-200 m.(300-600 ft). Even if they had, on seeing the tent still standing, they would have gone back.

Summary of the arguments against the avalanche theory:

- No traces of any avalanche were discovered.

- The only possible type of avalanche, on such a low-angled slope, could last for only several minutes without any danger of being repeated, while something kept the climbers away from the tent for quite a long time.

- Their belongings, such as aluminium cups and pails, were unbroken by any weight of snow. The pair of skis was standing in the snow untouched.

- These were experienced mountaineers, who knew that, to escape avalanches, in general one runs to the side, not further down the slope in the path of the avalanche.

# 2

The awfulness of the deaths has become part of a puzzle that has become more, not less, intriguing over time. Indeed, it's now a Russian national legend that has gone global. The American writer and film-maker, Donnie Eichar, in his engaging and widely-read book *Dead Mountain* proposes the infrasound theory. In fact, this theory was put forward in Russia some years ago, but never became popular. Eichar explores the infrasound phenomenon, a low-frequency sound wave effect which can be created by freakishly rare natural conditions and which causes dread and fear, nausea, and sometimes panic.

In his book, Eichar says there are apparently two types of wind phenomena which can create infrasound: a rolling change of wind direction, for instance as it comes over a hill, and a vortex like a tornado.

This theory says that the Dog Rock, which was located around a mile away, might have caused a wave to develop in those intense winds, and the downstream effects rolled over to the tent. American researchers of the physical phenomenon have subsequently ruled out the Dog Rock but they state that the shape of Otorten itself is perfect, and the tent was pitched at exactly the (possible) breaking point of the wavelength, where it would have devastated the students and caused them to run, thinking that the roaring originated from something like an express train that was running into them.

Eichar wrongly estimates the winds to have been around 40-60 miles per hour. This could have been the case on January 31 when the students themselves mentioned a very strong and warm westerly wind. But on February 1 the weather changed suddenly both in terms of temperature, humidity and wind speed/direction. Apart from the weather report found in the criminal case file, which stated the winds were only 1-3 m/s (3-6 mph), there is data from the three weather stations in the area: Troitsk-Pecherski, which is 123 miles north of Dyatlov Pass, Nyaksimvol (59 miles north-east) and Ivdel (75 miles south). The winds were reported on Februry 1: Nyaksimvol – 6 m/s, Ivdel – 5 m/s and Troitsk-Pecherski – 5.5 m/s which is around 12 mph.

Of course, none of the stations is on the same longitude with the place of the tragedy but we can use the average figures because careful analysis of the extended data indicates that there were no major distinctions in their weather reports during the key period. For instance, when on February 4 the temperatures really dropped, all three stations came in with very similar figures. Without going into too much detail on the influence of the wind's direction upon its speed when it comes about the slopes of a mountain range, we can look at yet other evidence, which is the footprints of the students themselves.

Modern experts say that the formation of the specific footprints (raised columns) observed on the slope could only have been possible if wind speeds had not exceeded 3-4 m/s (6.84 mph). There were several experiments done on the slope in 2013, performed under different wind and temperature conditions. They were sponsored by the Russian newspaper *Komsomolskaya Pravda*. The footprints mentioned could have formed under different temperature conditions, but only if there had been a snowfall that put at least 7 inches of fresh snow upon an older, firmer layer of snow underneath. It took approximately 15-17 hours for those raised footprints to form. Folks were walking and running in their socks and there were also rescue team members who walked around in their boots. Both left these raised footprints. But in less than a day they were obscured by the wind, which was 15-18 m/s. (33-40 mph). There are many factors involved in their preservation, such as the sun, the wind and the temperature. As Brustnitsyn earlier testified for the criminal case, some of those footprints can stay visible for the whole winter. The fact that the Dyatlov team's raised footprints were well preserved after almost a month suggests that the winds permitted sufficient time for them to get firm due to insolation and subsequent freezing. So the wind couldn't have been more than 3-4 m/s, which only confirms the weather report Lev Ivanov used. Thus there was no tornado-like vortex, and the shape of the landscape by itself was not enough to create this odd sound effect.

Also the footprints of the students don't suggest that they were running around in panic. There are multiple testimonies that they were walking rather than running and their footprints looked like parallel chains. Prosecutor Tempalov reported in his radio message: 'The footprints showed to me that the people were walking in regular strides.' We have even more impressive testimony from both Koptelov and Sharavin that before the students began their descent, they were standing for some time in one row, shoulder to shoulder.

This testimony was misused by the Discovery Channel in their TV special *Russian Yeti: The Killer Lives*, first aired in 2014. In the translation of Koptelov's testimony, one essential Russian word was omitted: ШЕРЕНГА which means 'people standing in line for attention', like in the Army. The TV special attributes this to a Yeti. Koptelov describes the prints as 'deep' because in the Russian language there is no equivalent word for 'imprinted'. The speaker just wanted to distinguish between imprinted and raised prints. They appear strange to him (and he certainly explained why he thought so, but he was cut off before he finished) because it seemed that the people were not walking but *standing*. Anyone can tell the difference between the footprints of a standing person from those of someone walking.

Another weak point of Eichar's approach is that the infrasound theory offers no possible explanation of the trauma of the bodies found in the ravine. In the Otorten region there are some snow-covered stones, including huge ones with different configurations, but as investigator Ivanov stated, these weren't in the path of the group members, and they certainly didn't launch themselves at anyone! Furthermore, according to rough estimates, the height from which the people would need to fall in order to suffer the impact observed, had to be at least 60 feet. The ravine is only nine feet deep. Again, the drop would affect the entire body and would be accompanied by fractures of the pelvic bones, limbs and head, along with rupturing of internal organs. There is no indication of any of these injuries in the post-mortem examination. Modern expert Eduard Tumanov, who is the most reputed forensic pathologist in Russia, has carefully studied the autopsy reports and discounted any possibility of a drop trauma in the bodies. The detailed analysis of the reports will follow towards the end of this book.

For now, we'll put aside natural factors due to the simple fact that there have been many other expeditions to the same place since then, with numerous hikers travelling off-road to Dyatlov Pass almost daily – some of them even pitching their tents at exactly the same place. None have perished in a similar way in the 50-plus years since the incident. It seems more credible that there must instead have been some singular situation that resulted in the deaths of the Dyatlov group.

# 3

What if the climbers had witnessed some secret trials or experiments that no one was supposed to see, and were deliberately liquidated by military forces? One of the advocates of this theory, a Yekaterinburg journalist named Gennady Kizilov, analysed all of the interrogation transcripts and statements of the witnesses and rescue team, and concluded that the whole rescue operation was a farce. He pointed out some major inconsistencies and conflicting testimony, and suggested that, a few days prior to the arrival of the search parties, other people were on the scene to prepare what was to be found by the search party. In order to avoid the disclosure of the secret facilities and to hide their crimes, the military and KGB removed the dead bodies from the real place of their death and brought them to slope 1079. Entries in the diaries of the group describing their route were then deliberately edited during the course of the investigation

Some rescuers and commentators say the tent was pitched in exactly the right manner, but others say that, to pitch the tent on the slope of the mountain when the trees were so close by was not the mark of experienced climbers, because it would have been exposed to the strongest of the gales in that area. They say the tent was pitched elsewhere but was then moved to the slope by unknown persons who wanted to create confusion.

According to this argument, the labaz was faked in a similar way. It was hurriedly created during the same period of time that the rescue team was already working. Indeed, the way the labaz itself was made looks as if it was constructed in haste – in a snow pit, rather than in trees beyond the reach of animals, as was more usual.

Some people also wonder about something else apparently found in the labaz: Dyatlov's boots. How could he have skied if he wasn't wearing his boots? Yudin's answer was that, with the semi-rigid 'soldiers' mount' (or bracing) that strapped over the top of the footwear, it was possible to ski in valenki and, moreover, Krivonischenko, for one, preferred to ski in these felt boots.

As for the extra skis found marking the labaz, and thought by some to have been accidentally left behind by someone other than the group, Yudin doesn't recall bringing any extra skis along on the trek.

But Yudin's memory isn't infallible. He has been interviewed many times by different people, and sometimes he makes mistakes. For instance, in one interview he stated he searched for minerals alone at the Second Severniy Settlement, but the diaries show that several students were involved in this.

Ski professionals say that extra pairs of skis are essential for such a long route. Traditionally, the last person in a procession dragged them behind with a rope. It was probably this extra pair that was used to make 'Kolevatov's sledge' mentioned in their spoof newspaper, the *Otorten Evening News*.

Furthermore, Slobtsov stated that when he first found the tent, he saw 'an extra pair of skis' there. Since he has a lot of experience in trekking and hiking, his lack of surprise implies it was natural to find that the group had extra skis.

It is true that at that time in the Soviet Union a variety of weapons was being developed – chemical, bacteriological, psychotronic, neutron, laser, vacuum, etc. However, to test these weapons, a specially equipped area with the right infrastructure, perimeter security, and personnel would have been needed. None of these were observed near Kholat Syakhl or Otorten.

Speculation even exists that the hikers were themselves deliberately chosen to be the test subjects of some experiment. This assumption is based on the later testimony of Lyudmila Vsevolzhskaya, who worked as a coach for a sports school in Serov, and who in 2009 told a researcher, Oleg Strauch, the following:

> My hiking group was scheduled to go to Mount Otorten after the group from the Ural Polytechnic Institute, which was Dyatlov's group. The Dyatlov group had already passed the town of Serov, and our group, which was to go after them, was delayed due to the late preparation of the documents needed to enter the route.
>
> A few days after the Dyatlov group passed Serov, I got a call from Sverdlovsk. I was told the route to Otorten was closed and we should cancel the hike. Of course, this news struck us like a thunderbolt. Why? However, we were not informed of the reasons. But the news that the Dyatlov group was lost only became public on February 12th, 1959, while we were told that we were not allowed on the route in late January or early February 1959!

These accounts are indeed confusing, and suggest that someone allowed one group to enter the area while another group was forbidden. Still, even if the Dyatlov group really had stumbled upon some big secret and had to be killed to prevent the story from leaking, or even if the group had been used for an experiment, the KGB would never have done it in this way.

Instead, the KGB would most likely have simply shot them, then removed the bodies in sealed coffins and issued a statement that the group members had, for example, eaten poisoned deer meat and were contaminated to the extent that no one could be allowed to see them. That was the ruthless way in which the KGB operated. In fact, in those times forcing the relatives to sign a confidentiality document on pain of life imprisonment would have ensured total silence. This would have been the preferred option for the KGB, avoiding the resources mobilised and the money and time expended on the search party.

These claims of a conspiracy are contradicted by one important fact: under Rustem Slobodin's corpse a 'death bed' was discovered. This is a feature that allows investigators to determine whether a person has died in the snow or was brought from somewhere else and thrown into the snow. Under a living person lying on the snow for a long time, the snow melts and turns to ice. This was the case with Slobodin.

Thus, because of the presence of this death bed, it must be said that Rustem, at least, died right on the slope and was not brought there post-mortem by someone else. The lack of a death bed under Dyatlov and Kolmogorova might indicate they fell to the snow at the moment their lives ended, having continued to walk until the very last moment.

When it comes about finding those responsible for terrible events, Russians and Americans never failed to blame each other. There is another theory that would provide material for a Hollywood blockbuster about a battle between good and evil during the Cold War.

A version of events has been suggested by Alexey Rakitin in which the Dyatlov expedition was under KGB supervision and three of the group's members were KGB agents: Zolotariov, Kolevatov and Krivonischenko. We'll cover this argument in more detail, since it's a fresh development, and has been discussed in a recent book on the case. This is considered by many to be the only possible scenario, since it explains the radioactive contamination of some parts of the clothes.

There are some facts of Zolotariov's biography which lend weight to the idea that he worked for the KGB. He studied at the Kharkov Institute of Physical Education, majoring as a fitness instructor at a women's school; however, the courses he took were anything but ladylike – fencing, boxing and wrestling. In those days, physical education institutes certainly did teach normal citizens, but also professionals of a completely different profile. Zolotariov had graduated from the Marx-Leninism Institute, which was completely unnecessary for a physical education instructor. The upheavals of his wartime front-line and personal lives in many ways speak to the likelihood of Zolotariov being a member of the KGB, in addition to the fact that he was buried separately from the rest of the group in a private ceremony.

According to this account, not long before the expedition, Krivonischenko was recruited by a foreign secret service. Using the expedition as a pretext, he promised to meet foreign spies in order to establish a connection and to give them some clothing impregnated with samples of radioactive materials. Thanks to testimony from a Congressional hearing, it is clear that by 1957 it was already known that radioactive dust had been given to the United States on a fur hat, which allowed them to determine the nature of the production at the closed city of Tomsk-7.

Russian writer, Alexey Rakitin, says this expedition could have been a very interesting opportunity for the intelligence services, since the data obtained from aerial photographic imagery and electric grid analysis – the assessments of plant efficiencies and, as a result, production capabilities – were very uncertain.

Reliable estimates of plant efficiency would have required detailed knowledge of Soviet gaseous diffusion technology and plant operations, which stand-alone collection systems simply couldn't deliver. This point was made by Oleg Bukharin (a Senior Security Specialist in the Office of Nuclear Security and Incident Response of the U.S. Nuclear Regulatory Commission) in his article 'The Cold War Atomic Intelligence Game, 1945-1970.'

Traditional human intelligence tradecraft was practically impossible to perform in this region, as it was completely closed to foreigners; it is not known whether or not attempts were made. In his article, Bukharin states: 'The lack of reliable on-the-ground intelligence made it difficult for the West to understand important developments inside the Soviet nuclear complex, which resulted in significant intelligence gaps.'

This could mean there were either no agents, the West didn't have agents they could trust, or the agents weren't well enough informed to provide accurate intelligence. When contacted, Bukharin declined to specify.

Assuming there were still some attempts to establish on-the-ground connections, the only possible way to get in touch with workers from closed enterprises would have been through agents using operatives without ties to the government for which they worked.

Such agents, or operatives, are typically abbreviated in espionage parlance to 'NOCs' (non-official cover). These agents are also known as 'illegals'. Agents with official cover – diplomatic immunity – are protected from the harsh punishments normally meted out to captured spies. Agents using unofficial cover do not have this safety net and, if captured or charged, could be subjected to severe criminal punishments, up to and including execution.

Agents using unofficial cover are also usually trained to deny any connection with their government, thus preserving plausible deniability, but also denying them any hope of diplomatic legal assistance or official acknowledgment of their service.

The Dyatlov expedition could have been used as part of an abortive exchange of secrets, planned to be completed in the wilderness, with the hope of escaping observation. To justify their appearance in such a remote area, it is postulated that NOCs disguised as geologists, after meeting with Krivonischenko, left Kholat Syakhl (1079) and headed west toward Komi, deep into Sverdlovsk Oblast (to the south), or to the east. And, in a place where inhabited settlements could be found only every 130-150 km (80-93 mi) in all directions, it would ideal for a group that has proper equipment and experience of living in winter conditions.

However, after the encounter took place, something went wrong. It might be that the NOCs somehow guessed that this group was not a bunch of innocent students or, vice versa, that the innocent part of the student group found that the spies were not acting like normal Russians, became suspicious, and the spies decided to terminate the operation and the participants.

People who were used as illegal anti-communist spies were often recruited from among Soviet 'migrs' like the veterans of the Vlasov Army. Examples are the notorious Organization of Ukrainian Nationalists known as 'Banderovtsi' (after their leader Stepan Bandera), and Eastern-Front SS collaborators etc.

Projects like Operation Bloodstone brought many of these people to the United States to serve as Cold War espionage assets.

On June 25, 2000, the *Los Angeles Times* published an article entitled 'The Nazi Past Underlying Politics Today'. The article cites Harry Rostizke, the ex-head of the CIA's Soviet desk:

> It was a visceral business of using any bastard as long as he was anti-Communist. The eagerness to enlist collaborators meant that you didn't look at their credentials too closely.

The Bloodstone project was active from 1948 to 1950, when similar programs under direct CIA sponsorship superseded it. On February 2, 2005 the *New York Times* published an article about the CIA refusing to turn over, to a Congressional working group, the documents in its possession relating to its relationship with Nazi war criminals.

So it is possible that these alleged agents were recruited from these kinds of people and that when the agents realised their plan wasn't working, they killed the members of the Dyatlov group in their customary manner.

This theory might explain why Zolotariov had a camera on his neck until the very moment of his death. It also explains the KGB presence during the search, because they wanted to see whether the clothes had been delivered or not. As Askinadze recalls, when the bodies of the rest of the group were found in the ravine, he felt the investigators had no real interest in the examination of all of these things. It would also explain why Ivanov ordered a radiological examination of the clothes and bodies, and why the clothes were contaminated but the bodies were not.

According to this version, the fireballs were illumination flares intended for the artificial lighting of the target area for reconnaissance purposes. The theory reads like a classic crime story, where there are good guys (the Dyatlov group) and bad (the spies).

Arguments against the espionage theory can be summarised as follows:

- The great difficulty of bringing spies to the slope and allowing them to leave it safely.
- It's not clear what kind of motives they had in killing all these 'KGB' agents, since, as soon as they were missed, their controllers would search for the spies.
- This is a theory of great complexity, so much so that the explanation appears 'stretched':
- Is it feasible that all this could have taken place so far in the wilderness, which both foreign spies and KGB personnel would find extreme and alien?
- The KGB would surely have given more support to their agents.

# 4

In analysing the awful details of the case, it is easy to feel that we are gazing into some hellish world of its own where normal logic ceases to apply, where the chain of cause and effect is broken, and where even common-sense notions of space and time are disregarded. As Lyuda's father wrote, 'I can't believe this happened in the Soviet Union.' He knew that the investigation hadn't found the answer, but he could not stop thinking that there must *be* an explanation.

He also wrote:

> From what I've heard among the university students, the escape of the undressed people from the tent was caused by an explosion and major radiation. No efforts were made to extinguish any fire. Also there was no sign of forest fire, and the colours of the body parts were different. Exposed skin was black and clothed areas were normal.

> Furthermore, the Communist Party official, Ermash, said to Kolevatov's sister that those whose bodies had not yet been found could not have survived for more than an hour-and-a-half. This makes me think that all this happened because of an explosion and radiation. This made the students flee, and possibly it affected their behaviour and even their sight. The university students say that very early on 2 February a group of climbers that were on another mountain, Chistop, observed a fireball. I think this so-called fireball was from outside the USSR.

That's why I'm surprised they had not closed the trekkers' routes out of Ivdel. I also think that, if the direction of the fireball deviated, and it never arrived at its destination, then in my opinion the authority responsible for its launch should have sent airborne explorers to trace its outcome and to alleviate any damage or injury among those that were affected.

If this wasn't done, then this was from the military, and it showed the same heartless disregard for the sanctity of life and for other people, such as the locals or hunters in this area. But in case this exploration was actually conducted, maybe they rescued the survivors. This is just my personal opinion and I have not discussed it with anyone else, because I'm aware this is not a matter for public dissemination.

This heart-breaking letter shows the stunning conscientiousness of many Soviet people who, despite feeling great personal pain, still took care, at least in print, to indicate respect for state secrets.

Zina Kolmogorova's sister, Tamara Zaprudina, was invited to take part in a TV show on the Dyatlov Pass incident in April 2013. She stated: 'I had another sister who's dead now; she was a member of the Party and went to the Party Committee, and they asked her "Are you a communist? What do you want here? If your parents need a pension, turn to the military. That's all."'

In later years, rocket launches from *Baikonur* Cosmodrome were shown on television, and some people guessed that a failed rocket launch could have been the cause of the tragedy. Their theory contends that because of some sort of defect, the rocket didn't achieve orbit and drifted back to Earth, travelling low above the tent and scaring the group.

A statement was made from the Cosmodrome, which is also called Tyuratam by intelligence services, and was the world's first and largest operational space launch facility. It is located in the desert steppe of Kazakhstan. The Cosmodrome management was asked many times whether it had fired or tested any rockets at the time of the incident, and they sent the following official statement to Vladimir Lebedev of the rescue team:

On those dates you have identified from 25 January to 5 February 1959 there were no ballistic or any other activities, and we can say for sure that the fall or crash of any rocket in the area you identify is impossible.

Multiple enquiries were made to the relevant government agencies to check whether any rocket launches had been conducted during that particular period of time. All received negative answers.

It's been said that a trajectory over the area of interest wouldn't have been used for rocket tests, as that would have involved rockets flying against the Earth's rotation, which is undesirable. In addition, there were there no military trials being conducted at the Kapustin Yar firing range in this area. Plisyetsk started functioning only in 1963.

Foreign observers such as NORAD (North American Aerospace Defence Command) have no record of a launch occurring from Baikonur between January 30 and February 3, 1959. However, this is not surprising, given that the US Air Force (namely, NORAD) was not given the role of global missile detection/monitoring until the 1960s.

In 1959, the United States Department of Defence approved the development of systems to track both manmade space objects and Soviet missiles in the form of ground-based radars dubbed 'PAVE PAWS' and 'BMEWS'. These radar systems didn't become operational until the early 1960s. In addition, Defence Support Program satellites, the other key system used for detecting launches and tracking missile trajectories, didn't come online until the 1970s.

It is known, however, that in 1957-1959 the USSR performed the first tests on the R-7 and R-12 ballistic missiles (the R-12 is known abroad as the SS-4 Sandal). R-7s were launched from Tyuratam and were programmed to fall on the Kura range in Kamchatka.

It may be a coincidence, but on February 17, 1959, when a thousand Ural residents saw something strange in the sky, the first R-7 rocket was launched from Tyuratam which is about 1200km (745 mi) south. After twenty-eight minutes, the R-7's warhead reached its target on Kura.

Could it have been possible for someone to see the launch of the R-7 from the outskirts of Ivdel and to have thought it was a UFO? This cannot be disregarded, as under the right conditions the effect of ballistic and space rockets can be seen for thousands of kilometres.

On March 31, another day when flying spheres were reported in the area, an R-7 was launched and was a failure.

It is possible that tests of further rockets were not disclosed in the public record. Indirect testimonies exist that show that some of the trials were not announced. 'Many years later, I spoke with scientists from Korolev's and Raushenbakh's circle,' said investigator Korotaev. 'It was intimated there were certain tests.'

The missing remains of the rocket, Yudin says, may still lie somewhere in the area or may have been removed by the special survey group mentioned in the letter from Lyuda's father.

According to this theory, the group died as a result of the shock wave from an explosion, causing serious bodily injuries to some of them (presumably those who at the moment were standing) and chemical poisoning. Indirect evidence of this is the unusual skin colour and possible vision problems.

It is necessary to mention that blast injury is also a complex type of physical trauma and has its own specific signs that are very well-defined in related research. In this case, however, none were observed.

The idea that it was the military that should be blamed for what happened still persists in Yekaterinburg today. In the city, not only experts in the case, but a wide variety of people, from taxi drivers to scientists, still assert that misplaced zeal for National Security was the cause.

However, there was one man who never believed in conspiracy or military test theories. This man was Lev Ivanov. Finally, he spoke up...

# 5

Many years after the incident, retired and residing in Kazakhstan, Ivanov gave a long and very strange interview to a local newspaper, *The Way of Lenin*, a substantial portion of which is presented here:

We are now used to the fact that some newspapers, in their search for sensationalistic scandals, will publish unverified and sometimes untrustworthy information. I was interested in an article in the newspaper *The Way of Lenin*. The publication was about UFOs as they appear in the American press. I was particularly impressed by the trustworthiness of this because, as it is fairly written, the authorities sometimes suppress obvious facts about UFOs. This is indeed true and I would like to tell you about how [they do it].

Thirty years ago I dealt with this myself while working as an official. But in my case the circumstances were very tragic. Everything I will tell you is backed up by official records, which are now kept at the State Archives of the Yekaterinburg region. For that reason I will change neither the last names nor the dates of the incident. In the information I give, there will be no artistic license; the fact is absolutely documented and was published and presented to the public thirty years later, under the initiative of the editors of the newspaper *Ural Worker*.

By the end of January 1959, a group of sports skiers went on an expedition aiming for Mount Otorten, which is situated north of Ivdel in the upper reaches of the River Auspiya. All of the climbers died; everyone was told that the hikers found themselves in an extreme situation and froze to death. But it was not true. The real causes of death were hidden from people. Just a few people were familiar with the real story. These were the Secretary of the regional Communist Party, Kirilienko; his Deputy Head, Yeshtorkin; the Regional Prosecutor, Klinoff, and the author of this article who was investigating the case. Today none of the others are alive.

What I want to talk about are some mysterious phenomena that time after time occur on Planet Earth, which no one has been able to explain so far. What caused the tourists to flee the tent? There are no insignificant things in an investigation.

Next to the tent there was a natural sign that one man had left the tent to relieve himself. He had gone out without footwear and then the same footprint without footwear was seen still without boots down in the valley. There was every reason to guess this same person had raised the alarm and had no time to put on his footwear.

This means there was something scary that not only alarmed him, but [also] made all the others leave the tent urgently and seek shelter lower down in the taiga. To find this force, or at least to get closer to it, was the aim of the investigation.

On 26 February 1959, at the edge of the taiga we found the remains of a small fire, and here we found Doroshenko's and Krivonischenko's bodies in their underwear. Then in the direction of the tent we found Dyatlov's body and two more – Slobodin and Kolmogorova. I have to say, the last three were the most physically whole and easily identifiable. They had been crawling from the fire to the tent for their clothes. It was absolutely obvious judging by their body positions.

On the last four bodies there was no external bruising or contusions; thus, there was a directed force, which selectively acted towards some of them, whilst excluding the others. There were some circumstances I want to tell you about now.

When, in May, Maslennikov and I were examining the scene we discovered that some young fir trees on the edge of the forest had traces of burning, but these traces had no concentric shape or system; there was no epicentre. These confirmed the direction of this force, which was a kind of a ray of warmth, or a very strong, but completely unknown, form of energy, which acted selectively. The snow was not melted. The trees were not damaged. I got the impression that after the tourists had walked, on their own legs more than 500 m (1640 ft) down the slope, some of them were targeted.

Nowadays we talk a lot about the 1950s, trying to make someone responsible for our past. It was a period of really strict discipline, especially in the area of law enforcement and officialdom. There were no ogres like Beria [Stalin's enforcer], but his culture was everywhere so, along with the prosecutor of the region, I reported our initial data to the Secretary of the local Communist Party, Kirilienko, and he gave me a very distinct order: make all the work secret, and not one word of information was to be released.

In addition, Kirilienko ordered us to bury the tourists in closed coffins and to tell the relatives they had frozen to death. The accident was reported to Khrushchev, and as we know from one correspondent of this newspaper who was part of the rescue team, he ordered that there should be no reports until the investigation was complete and all the bodies had been found.

And when we had found all the bodies and some details emerged which I described above, Kirilienko decided not to inform Khrushchev. The whole situation was dropped at a high level and all of the relatives' enquiries were ignored. That is how our country was at the time, and it was not we who created this culture.

In fact, whilst the investigation was still open, the newspaper *Tagil Worker* carried a very tiny note that a globe of fire – or a UFO, as we now say – was detected on Mount Otorten. This UFO was moving noiselessly in the direction of the northern Ural Mountains. The reporter of this piece asked: what could it be? For this infringement, the editor of the paper was punished, and I was advised not to dig deeper.

The overseer of my investigation was Yeshtokin, the Deputy Head of the local Communist Party. At the time we all knew little of UFOs and radiation. The ban on these topics was [to prevent] the off-chance of even a random decryption of material related to rocket missile projects and nuclear technology, the development of which was just beginning at that time. The world was in the period of the Cold War.

But I still had to somehow conduct an investigation. I am a professional, and I had to somehow find the answer. I decided to keep investigating despite this ban, because the other versions [of the incident] involving attacks by people, animals and storms had been excluded by the data to which I had access, and it was clear to me how they died, and in what order, and in which circumstances. This was revealed by the diligent examination of the bodies, clothes, etc. Thus, it was only the sky, and what was in the sky, that remained as an explanation.

There was an energy we did not know, an energy that was beyond human strength. So, along with scientists from the Ural Scientific Academy, I made some serious examinations of the clothes and certain organs of the dead people to check whether there was radiation. To compare these results, we also took the clothes and organs of the people who had died in a natural way or in road accidents.

The data we obtained indicated the presence of radioactive 'mud' or dust that could be rinsed by water. Before these bodies were found, they had been intensely rinsed by the water under the snow; therefore, at the moment of their deaths, the concentration of radioactive 'mud' was many, many times higher.

As a prosecutor, who at the time had already had experience of working on some secret defence matters, I dismissed the suggestion of nuclear weapons trials in this area. I looked very closely at the reports of fiery globes. I questioned many eyewitnesses who saw this UFO in the sub-polar Urals. By the way, I do not mean that these UFOs are connected with aliens. A UFO is an unidentified flying object, and that's it. A lot of data speaks of the fact that [the UFOs] can be bursts of energy not understood by modern science, but which affect life and the environment.

Re-examining the case, I am now more than ever convinced it was a UFO, as I concluded back then.

On the basis of the data obtained, the role of a UFO in this tragedy is absolutely obvious. It was already written in [the Russian] press that even myself, as a prosecutor and criminalist, tried to stress that the real cause of the death of people was an Unidentified Flying Object, although I hid this in my final conclusion, by using the words 'an impact of an overwhelming force.'

When asked if I have changed my opinion over the past 30 years, I would say I have changed only my view of the technical aspects of the impact. If I previously believed the globe exploded and showered unidentified radioactive energy over the area, now I think this energy from the globe was directed, and aimed at just three people.

When I reported to Yeshtokin on all these findings, like beaming globes, radioactivity, etc., he gave me absolutely clear orders: make everything secret, put all the documents in a sealed package, bring it to the security archives, and forget about it.

Needless to say, everything was done exactly so.

To a modern reader, this could appear strange: what was the big secret? But please try to remember that, immediately before this accident, there was a so-called radioactive discharge in Kyshtym. We can talk about it now, and read about it in newspapers, but anyone who tried to discuss it then? No one would dare. [This becomes clearer] when you consider that, in the contamination zone in the Kyshtym region, a massive number of people knew the real situation. And those who knew were silent.

Older generations will recall what kind of times these were; it was only recently that satellites were sent into space. Back then there were some trials of nuclear and hydrogen bombs, and many people made the connection between UFOs [and] decontamination efforts.

But the data of our investigation indicated that the case of the Dyatlov group had nothing to do with any military trials. Today, when everyone knows about the test areas and the methods of testing nuclear bombs, our version of the deaths of [these] people has been even more confirmed. The modern generation should not judge us too harshly.

I am not trying to justify that I covered up all of the material about the fireball, nor that how so many people died was kept secret. I asked the editor to publish my apologies to the relatives of the dead for my hiding of the truth from them. But four times no space could be made! So I take my chance in getting it published here, and I hereby apologise again to the families of the dead, especially Dubinina, Tibo, and Zolotariov. I am sorry. I tried to do what I could, but at that time in this country there was an overwhelming force.

# 6

Many people, of course, would simply not regard these comments as having any serious merit because Ivanov mentioned Unidentified Flying Objects (UFOs) and their possible relevance to the case. But the fact that Ivanov is a major figure in the investigation into the mystery of the Dyatlov group makes his interview of great importance.

That there was definitely something going on in the sky that very night is pretty obvious. Krivonischenko's camera was found attached to the tripod which means that he was going to take a shot of something very important. The last picture taken (frame 34) shows a glowing object leaving a luminous trail. In the centre of the shot we see the usual glare from a bright object. The curved band at the bottom is a technical defect in the film.

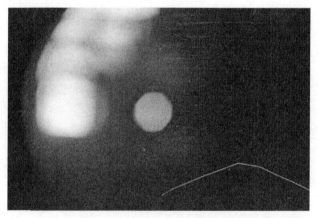

The 34th frame

Some have speculated that the photograph was taken with a standard Zorkiy Industar-22 as in bright specks eight borders are clearly seen and there are the eight petals of the diaphragm of the lens. The photo was taken with a covered diaphragm and most likely not with an extended tube. This supports the assumption that the frame was randomly taken by a forensic expert to rewind the film back into the case, as the unit was stored loaded.

There is another theory that Krivonischenko probably saw something unusual in the sky and in the excitement of the moment he didn't have time to verify the full extraction of the lens. Thus, even if the object was very far away and he correctly set the focus to infinite the picture would be blurred. The shot was most likely taken in an open area during the night, and not in some sort of building, as the strong light from the object would have partially illuminated what was inside. There is nothing like that in the photograph.

There is also one more 'last shot' found in another film. Boris Bychkov (a fellow UPI student who was a friend of the group) was given all the film from the group's cameras to develop in the Ural Technical University's laboratory. Bychkov says that he saw the full films before they were cut into pieces of six to seven pictures. One of these pictures shows a shot taken by the Dyatlov group themselves, and then another of their dead bodies in the morgue. Apparently the same camera was used by the Dyatlov group as well as by those who were present in the morgue. This was a completely normal situation for those years, when people used what was at hand to take photographs. When the film was cut into several pieces, the 26th shot was together with the photograph of the dead bodies. This occurred because at the time Bychkov did not pay attention to the frame, as he considered it to be spoiled.

Thus, the last frame made on the mountain slope became the first in the cutting from the morgue. Thus it turns out that both final frames – the 34th frame from Krivonishenko's film and the 26th frame from this film (assumed to be Slobodin's) – captured some sort of glowing object. In the first example, the shot was taken with a tripod; the second was taken by hand and is thus blurred.

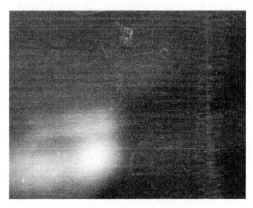

The 26th frame of Slobodin's film

Recently attention was drawn to the plain dark frames from the other cameras. These frames are numerous (around 30 altogether) and when zoomed up to hundreds of times they look like this:

One of the many frames that appear as "plain dark" ones and look like this one after considerable zooming up

It seems that the students kept taking pictures. Considering the number of the shots taken, the event lasted at least one-and-a-half to two minutes, which also means it was very far from the group, perhaps 300 km (186 mi) away, and thus couldn't hurt them. Had the objects been closer to the tent, they would have been observed just for several seconds before they were gone beyond the pass and we wouldn't have had these 30 shots. Possibly this excludes the rocket theory.

In his subsequent testimony Nicolai Kuzminov, who took part in the rescue operation, recalled that, on one of the nights, he and the rest of the party observed this phenomenon. 'The next day after this "incident," we sent a radio message requesting our immediate removal from the search zone. We received an answer that this was a test of a new form of hydrogen fuel and was not life threatening, we just needed to stay in the tent when we saw it. They promised to stop the tests during the search. We calmed down and continued searching.'

Of course, this could be an explanation for the strange phenomena aimed at preventing any panic or disobedience from the rescue team. But again we see that there was no danger for them.

The second explanation is that it was a celestial body and that it was similar in appearance to that which occurred at Chelyabinsk on February 15, 2013. It should be noted that, if we speculate that a complex or 'cluster' of bodies are moving in almost the same orbit, with some of them hitting the Earth at one date and the others at later times (which provides a possible explanation for the suspicious coincidence of conditions) the date of impact should always be close to the passage of the Earth through the nodes of the complex orbit.

This explains why certain meteor showers occur during the exact same month and days every year (for example, the Leonids in November and the Perseids in August, which are among the most intense meteor showers of the year). Also in the case of a major meteor shower the 'radiant' (the point from where the majority of meteors appear to come from in the sky) is the same every year.

Regardless, the fact that the impacts came from almost the same direction in the sky and hit the Earth just 2400 km (1491 mi) from Chelyabinsk might be too surprising to be a coincidence.

But there are several things that don't fit this theory. The time during which the 'fiery balls' were seen is one of them. Minutes are not a typical time scale of these phenomena. Given that velocities are in the wide range of 10 to 70 km/s (6-43 mi/s), even in the high atmosphere the display could not have lasted more than a few seconds. The time of the whole visual phenomenon at Chelyabinsk, for example, was no more than ten seconds, although the contrail, the arrival of the blast wave, and the dissipation of the cloud took several minutes.

In exploring the information derived from the Chelyabinsk event, it's difficult to determine the likelihood that the same meteorite complex was also associated with a huge meteor shower in 1959. That is too long ago to allow for a reliable prediction based merely on the available information about the orbit of the Chelyabinsk Event Impactor (CHEI); however, based on statistics it's still theoretically possible, according to Jorge Zuluaga, head of the undergraduate program in astronomy at the University of Antioquia.

One of the witnesses describes an azimuth and elevation of the bodies that are similar to the Tunguska and Chelyabinsk events: both came from east-southeast and the radiant was not higher than 30 degrees. This implies a very shallow impact within the atmosphere, and with the potential to heat any meteoroid and produce an airburst such as that observed in Chelyabinsk.

Until now, an airburst has been understood as occurring only if the object has low density and is fragile, which was why the Tunguska impactor is thought to be a fragment of a comet. Chelyabinsk, with its clear asteroidal orbit, and the finding of fragments after the event, showed that large rocky bodies can explode without impacting the ground.

The blast wave could have broken the branches of the cedar, because testimony also exists from a member of the rescue party that some young fir trees around the cedar tree had lightly burned needles.

The interpretations of the phenomena observed in the sky on that night can be different but it is obvious that it drew Ivanov's attention. And what we should note from his interview is that Moscow didn't know what really happened. Kirilenko (a Local Communist Party Leader) informed Khrushchev because the incident took place in an area of potential interest to foreign intelligence, and the authorities had to be informed of the massive rescue operation there. Khrushchev simply forbade the release of any information until the investigation was complete and all the bodies had been found.

It is normal practice not to give out any information beforehand. Ivanov continues:

And when we had found all the bodies and some details emerged which I described above, Kirilienko decided not to inform Khrushchev.

So this was a totally local initiative in order to protect the regional bureaucrats from a random mistake so that they could keep their positions.

When I reported to Yeshtokin about all these findings, like beaming globes, radioactivity, etc., he gave me absolutely clear orders: make everything secret, put all the documents in a sealed package, bring it to the security archives, and forget about it.

Why? The answer is again found in Ivanov's letter.

The ban on these topics was [to prevent] the off-chance of even a random decryption of material related to rocket missile projects and nuclear technology, the development of which was just beginning at that time. The world was in the period of the Cold War.

Here is a simple answer to all the secrecy. But if the conspiracy hypothesis is not correct, then why was the KGB present during the search? To understand this, we must look more closely at the backgrounds of certain group members.

At least three group members worked, or had worked, at secret enterprises, and two of them even lived in so-called 'closed' or nuclear cities. These cities didn't appear on maps and were built in densely forested areas, primarily located in the Urals and Western Siberia. In non-secret documents, they were assigned the names of nearby towns and a numerical suffix. The use of post-box numbers for these towns continued until the early 1990s.

Krivonischenko worked at Chelyabinsk-40, which was involved in plutonium production and the manufacturing of nuclear components. The CIA knew of this town as Kyshtym. The main purpose of all this secrecy was to conceal operations from foreign spies and to increase survivability in the event of nuclear bombardment.

The isolation of personnel working in these facilities was done to prevent potential recruitment by foreign intelligence agencies and was a critical security task. The directors of the facilities, in coordination with the KGB, could grant permission to selected workers to leave their cities for vacation, medical treatment or study. Nonetheless, workers willing to spend their vacation inside a city received bonuses amounting to 50 percent of their monthly salaries.

All travellers had to have their travel routes approved and to sign non-disclosure agreements. There's an official letter, written by the authorities of the Ural Polytechnic Institute, asking the Chelyabinsk-40 management to allow Rustem Slobodin to take part in the Dyatlov expedition and grant him permission to leave the site.

Finding all the bodies was vital for Moscow and the local authorities. What if the group had indeed planned to escape with the information they had? These individuals could have escaped to Norway, after all. That is why the KGB was present during the search.

The cost of the search operations was very high. As noted earlier, there is an official letter from Nicolai Klinoff, the Prosecutor of Sverdlovsk region, to S.A. Golunskim, the Director of the National Institution of Research in Criminology, which states:

The enormous expenses being spent on the search may keep growing if no new method of searching for the corpses is applied. We know that your institution planned to create a device for spotting bodies buried underground using ultrasound. We heard there were some successful results when the device was used in similar situations. We think it would be reasonable to let us try to use such a device in our current search.

The institute issued an official reply stating that they didn't have a device such as this.

When all the bodies were found, the KGB lost interest and local Communist Party leaders rushed to finish the whole story for the reasons mentioned earlier: 'In addition, Kirilienko ordered us to bury the tourists in closed coffins and to tell the relatives they had frozen to death.'

So the investigation's statement that the students perished as the result of an 'overwhelming force' was thanks to Ivanov, whose conscience was unwilling to give 'freezing' as the reason for the deaths.

# PART V: THE 'OVERWHELMING FORCE'

# 1

It is said that the dead tell no lies, and this is a good reason to look more closely at the autopsy reports.

Forensic pathologist, Boris Vozrozhdenny, supposedly conducted the autopsies on the bodies in Ivdel. Unlike other participants in the events, he never talked to the press about it even many years after. The only known remark of his is what he said to Sergey Sogrin after he performed the autopsies on the corpses of the first group members found. 'Zina ... Such a beautiful, healthy girl, who could have lived and loved somebody and given birth to her children. So sad.'

Later, he received a lot of criticism for the job he did; for example, he didn't always differentiate between the injuries received while the person was alive and those that may have occurred later. The reports also lack many specific details and just replicate each other in their conclusive parts related to the cause of the deaths. This is no wonder considering that the coroner was given the task of concluding that the Dyatlov group froze to death. He was supervised by Prosecutor Klinov, who was present at the autopsies of the first five bodies.

In 2014, modern forensic expert Eduard Tumanov, the most respected and experienced coroner in Russia, studied the material and found a number of mistakes and incorrect conclusions.

For instance, the signs of death by freezing have been studied for a long time, especially in a cold country like Russia. Tomsk University Press published an informative book on the subject by V.P. Desyatov, titled *Death by Hypothermia* (1977). In it, Desyatov provides several interesting case studies:

Here is the case of Y.M. Rassokhin and L.P. Sokov (1966).

Patient G., thirty-three years old, was admitted to the hospital on 23 January 1964. A doctor picked him up off the street, hesitating as he debated whether to take him to a morgue or a hospital, and 'just in case' decided to bring him to a clinic. The limbs [of the body] were bent at the joints and could not be straightened out – the body was 'stiff'. The rectal temperature was below 0 C. Heartbeat, breathing and reflexes were completely absent. Direct cardiac massage and intra transfusion were started.

After twenty-five minutes, there was ventricular fibrillation of the heart. After forty minutes, breathing appeared. After fifty minutes, weak contractions of the heart began. After three hours and twenty-five minutes, the patient regained consciousness and started to talk. He remembered that having finished work, he drank a bottle of vodka and went home. The air temperature was -29C (-20F). He had been lying on the street for seven hours. There was no evidence of damage to the central nervous system (CNS), and one year later the patient's condition remained good.

The main sign of death from hypothermia is the presence of the so-called 'Vishnevsky spots,' described in 1895 by the coroner S.M. Vishnevsky. These spots are found on the gastric mucosa (stomach membrane) in about seventy-five percent of deaths from low temperatures. According to Vozrozhdenny, all members of the Dyatlov group had Vishnevsky spots. Tumanov questions the possibility of identifying these spots in the last four bodies due to the state of their deep decay; and even for the first five corpses, which were found in a much more preserved condition, it is difficult to give a clear hypothermia diagnosis based on this and other characteristic features of the condition. Tumanov also doubts the possibility of identifying oedema of the brain – one more characteristic of hypothermia. The brain matter in the corpses was 'a greenish red, jelly-like substance. The grey matter can hardly be distinguished from the white matter. Brain ventricle contours are indistinguishable. The cerebellum matter pattern is poorly distinguished.'

It was improper defrosting that made it impossible to diagnose oedema of the brain. Still Vozrozhdenny cited it in order to conclude that freezing was the cause of death. He also mentioned cardiac cavities full of liquid dark blood, which cannot qualify as a sign of death from hypothermia because the blood of frozen people is bright red due to high concentrations of oxyhemoglobin.

Finally, neither third nor fourth degree frostbite of fingers or toes was observed. Krivonischenko's report reads 'terminal phalanx is dry and dark brown in colour.' According to modern experts, these are the signs of post mortem freezing of the body.

Five of the group members had facial abrasions. Small abrasions often occur when an exhausted person is crawling in frozen conditions when he or she can injure the skin by rubbing against firm snow or ice. The location of these on the frontal parts of the bodies (faces and hands) excludes possible compression with snow (like in an avalanche). Had this been the case, they would have been observed all over the body evenly.

The bodies were not found in the classic foetal position supposedly assumed by a person freezing to death. Doroshenko and Krivonischenko were even found in a pose similar to that of sunbathing on a beach. In fact, the foetal position is found in less than 30% of all cases of death by freezing, and simply suggests that the person still felt cold when he or she died. Dyatlov's pose is closer to this classical position. Tumanov suggests that Dyatlov was the only one on the slope who really died by hypothermia.

There is another key question regarding the positions of the corpses: that of the post-mortem phenomenon called livor mortis.

Livor mortis usually starts twenty minutes to three hours after death and is congealed in the capillaries in four to five hours. Maximum lividity occurs within six to twelve hours. The blood pools in certain tissues of the body. The intensity of the colour depends upon the amount of reduced haemoglobin in the blood. The discolouration does not occur in the areas of the body that are in contact with the ground or another object, when the capillaries are compressed. As the vessel wall slowly becomes permeable due to decomposition, blood leaks through and stains the tissue.

Livor mortis in those who die of hypothermia is no different from that following death by other causes: it is still located in the lower parts of the body. Doctors know that the freezing of a corpse and its subsequent defrosting cannot change the location of livor mortis – it's simply impossible.

The livor mortis on three of the group members was not aligned with the position of the bodies at the scene; so the bodies were inverted, moved and possibly searched, and this happened not earlier than one day after the incident.

Doroshenko and Kolmogrova were found with their faces down while their livor mortis suggests that they died in different positions. The same was observed with Dyatlov

# 2

If we put together what Ivanov wrote in his article and his first impression that the Dyatlov team members had all been murdered, it is logical to suggest that the fireballs are somehow related to the murder.

Any guess as to the nature of these surreal objects, including UFOs, is confronted by pretty clear evidence in the autopsy reports that there was a fight. It implies that the attackers were visible for the group, that they were flesh and blood. As the forensic pathologist wrote:

> [Rustem's] fingers are clenched into a fist. In the area of the wrist joint of the hand there is a graze wound protruding from the soft tissue in an area 8 x 1.5 cm (3.5 x 0.19") in size covered in dry parchment-density crust under the layer of skin. In other words, the knuckles on both hands were skinned and had 'scabbed over.'

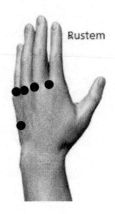

Rustem

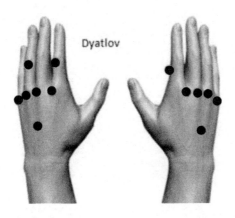

Dyatlov

Coroner Tumanov gives another example with Igor Dyatlov.

In the area of the wrist joints and between the phalangeal joints the soft tissue is of brown purple colour of parchment density covered by dry crusts with haemorrhaging into the underlying tissues.

Moreover, in the area of the palm surface of the second and fifth fingers there is a skin wound of irregular linear shape with regular edges located transverse to the length of the fingers; the surface wounds are up to 0.1-0.2 cm (0.5") deep. It's a cut, and it looks like Igor got it while trying to get a knife out of somebody's hand.

The same is observed with Zina's fists. She even had 'an irregularly shaped 3 x 2.2-cm (1.3 x 0.5") wound on the base of the third finger on the right hand with an angle facing the terminal phalanx with uneven borders and a scalped skin graft'. Coroner Tumanov is pretty positive that it was a mark caused by punching someone's teeth.

# Zina

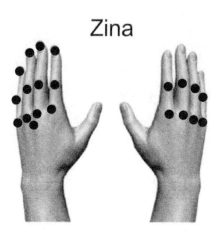

# Krivonischenko

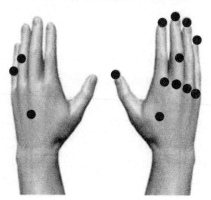

There are also marks of beating on the face of Doroshenko: the upper lip is swollen, and around the vermilion border of the upper lip, there is a 1.5 x 2 cm (0.19 x 0.5") dark red haemorrhage.

With regard to Krivonischenko:

> In the middle part of the brow there is a round contusion with a size of 0.3 x 0.3 cm. (0.5"), brown-red colour and with parchment density. In the left temporal area are two abrasions: grazes of brown-red colour with sizes of 1.2 x 0.3 cm (0.19 x 0.5") and 1 x 0.2 cm.

It is very unlikely that these contusions were caused by falling face down. Had this been the case, the graze wounds would also have been observed on his nose and above his eyebrows. There would have been more scratches on the forehead. What we see here is the result of a blow with a hard blunt impactor at an acute angle, according to Tumanov. His overall conclusion based on the nature of the injuries is that the murderers were not professionals and that the students were killed "unskillfully".

Whatever was observed in the sky could have made the students flee their tent, but it couldn't have fought with them. Who *did* they fight with in such a remote area, given the absence of footprints of any other party?

# 3

Let's remember that all the footprints on the slope, including those of the students, were only preserved in fragments. According to a radio message sent by the search team operator after the ski tracks were found:

It's a good trail made by a number of people, and is probably 10-15 days old, very easy to follow in the forest, but almost invisible in open places. The track goes to the ridge, where of course it disappears due to wind and snow drifts.

According to Atmanaki:

There were no footprints right around the tent because when the Dyatlov group dug they had stacked the snow all around, and later this snow was drifted by the wind, thus covering all the tracks. But thirty or forty metres down there was a file of very well-preserved footprints.

The Dyatlov group had gone in and out of the tent, hardening the ground; consequently, no tracks had been preserved next to the tent. Chernyshov also confirms that the footprints were only visible 40 m (131 ft) away (some say 30 and Sharavin says 7-10). These footprints disappeared again after approximately 500 m (0.3 mi) and were found again closer to the cedar.

There an experienced taiga ranger, Captain Chernyshov, noticed a footprint made by a shoe with a heel or by boots. Other members of the search party also noticed this. But this puzzle was solved in May, when Zolotarev's body was found. He had footwear with a heel.

Right around the cedar, again, it was hard to distinguish between the footprints because, according to Atmanaki, 'the snow around was trampled.'

Just as the Dyatlov group didn't leave any ski tracks on the slope, neither did the killers: the trails would have been destroyed by wind and snow.

Then there was a sheath found under the snow and later identified as having come from Kolevatov's knife, referred to in Ortukov's radio message from the search team: 'On the site of the tent we found an 18-cm-long scabbard or sheath, and one spoon. Supposedly this sheath belonged to Kolevatov.' It was an incorrect assumption because Kolevatov's Finnish knife was later discovered in the tent, still in its black leather sheath. In fact, all three Finnish knives were in the tent. Tibo's and Krivonishenko's knives were found in the pockets of their tarpaulin (CC, Vol 2, p.41). A 'tarpaulin' is a wind proof jacket, which would imply that the knives had never left the tent.

Captain Chernyshov stated: 'It's possible to surmise that other people had since been by the fire … The trees near the fire had been cut with knives, but we found no knives with the bodies.'

In his closing statement, Lev Ivanov, however, mentioned Krivonischenko's knife as a possible tool for cutting the trees and stated that it was found in the ravine next to the last four bodies. This is inconsistent not only with the criminal case entries mentioned above but also with the Scene Inspection Report dated May 6th, 1959, which goes into great detail about everything found there, including the number and kinds of trees as well as clothing, but never mentions any knives having been found. The document was signed by prosecutor Tempalov and several others, including Askinadze who is still alive and testified about what they had seen there. (CC Vol. 1 pp. 341-343). One can guess that Lev Ivanov had a commitment to close the case at any cost and so he made this evidence up in order to explain the situation with the tree pad.

Under the cedar, the search team found a kind of fabric belt of dark colour with some ties at the ends. An eyewitness said that it looked like one of the straps which the Mansi use for dragging loads, but not exactly the same because it was not as robust.

And, finally, there is an interview with Captain Chernyshov, which reads, in part:

Question: Were there any other prints of animals next to the tent, or next to the bodies?

Answer: No, none. I didn't see any wolf or dog prints myself. Yes, there was one track a long way from the tent, next to some stones, but it was the print from our search dog.

Question: Was it possible someone approached the tent without leaving tracks? For instance, the Mansi? Could they have got there with or without prints?

Answer: If the Mansi approached the tent on their skis, they would never have left prints. The slope above the tent is bare. Their skis wouldn't leave prints up there.

There must have been those who were at home in the snowbound, bitter taiga; mountain men who knew everything about tracking in the woods and on the slopes.

# 4

The final entry in the group's expedition diary, made by Dyatlov, concerns the Mansi and shows Dyatlov's powers of deduction from trail tracks and Mansi tree signs left behind for other Mansi:

> We're going along the well-trodden Mansi ski path. (Up to now we've travelled along a Mansi path, which not long ago was also used by a hunter on the back of a reindeer.) Yesterday we came upon his overnight shelter. The reindeer didn't go any further; the hunter himself did go further along the channel of the old trail, whose path we follow now.

The signs on the trees usually contain information about the hunt: the number of hunters, dogs and which animal have been killed

Where was 'the hunter' heading, given that 'the mountain where the group died is considered by the Mansi as not worthy for hunting and reindeer', as Lev Ivanov stated, giving one of the reasons for officially rejecting the Mansi as murderers. Clearly whether it was a mistake in the investigation, or the Mansi explored the area for other purposes, their tracks were in close proximity.

Both investigators, Lev Ivanov and Vladimir Korotaev, later testified that the discovery that the tent had been cut from the inside was the main reason to clear the Mansi of all suspicion.

Modern experts, however, express some doubts about the accuracy of this conclusion and the expertise of the investigators. Having scrutinized the full criminal case on the Dyatlov group, Natalia Sakharova, a criminal expert with 25 years of service, says there had to be at least two experts according to the procedure.

In this particular case the examination was performed at a very low professional level. There is no general photo of the tent stretched out in the laboratory to be examined. The diagram of the damage doesn't fit its actual location on the tent; there is no detailed description of the inner and outer sides (burns, scratches, traces of mending, blood). The damage is described selectively, which is a serious violation because it distorts the general picture of the traces; there are no descriptions of common signs of damage which would allow the grouping of the signs in order to define the group characteristics for the tools used (knives or ice breaker). There is no description of general signs for the tears, the direction (or angle) of force applied (from inside or outside); no description of the initial point of the impact (from which the cut or tearing started); no microscope photography to confirm the main point that the cuts were made from the inside. There is no such photography in the criminal case. And this forensic technique has been in full use since the 1930s! There is no reliable description of what was seen through the microscope: the direction of the scarf parts of the cuts, the separation of their fibres, or the direction of the thread sockets. Nothing at all! I think the expert didn't use the microscope because for this she would have had to dissect part of the fabric and enter a relevant record about it in her report. What is also extremely unusual is that they didn't invite any experts to view the place of occurrence. It is also important to mention that there were no expert experiments performed with the same kind of tent. They should have cut a tent from the inside in exactly the same way and then have several people exit it in order to see if it is possible to exit the tent in this way at all, and how it would affect the tent. Would it fall, or spring back, or remain standing? This kind of experiment usually proves or disproves a theory of the investigation. It was never done. Why? It was absolutely not OK to come to any conclusion based on just visual examination. The very fact that they used this inexperienced and poorly trained 'expert' is an alerting sign for me because the results of the expertise were crucial for the whole case. (1)

Even if the conclusion that the tent was cut from inside is correct, one possible explanation could be that somebody first scared or enticed the students out of the tent, then occupied it for a while, making sure the students couldn't return before they froze outside. Or more simply, the hunters could have cut the tent from the inside before they escorted the students away.

The investigation rejected the theory of the Mansi as murderers very quickly, stating: 'The investigation didn't find any signs of other people being on Summit 1079 except for the Dyatlov team on the first or second of February. The Mansi are usually friendly and provide tourists with places to sleep and assistance.'

A correction in the original text is visible here (right): the words for 'friendship' and 'overnight lodging' have been written over another phrase, 'in the absence of selfish or religious motives'. Certainly the presence of religious motives was hard to prove.

Later testimonies revealed that the area which the hikers had entered was actually a sacred place for the Mansi despite how often, during the investigation, both the Mansi and the locals testified that it wasn't. One of the most trustworthy testimonies is by the journalist, Gennady Grygoryev, who was familiar with both the Anyamov and the Bakhtiyarov Mansi families prior to the tragedy, and who spent much time talking to Kourikov. In an interview with Denis Milkov in 2012, he said: 'The Mansi told me that the mountain where they found the tent was a sacred place. They offered prayers at the bottom. The sacred area of the mountain is not as we would assume, with temples and idols, but merely land.'

Ivan Pashin, the local hunter-guide, originally refused to escort Slobtsov and Sharavin to the tent and, it was said, only after the shaman Kourikov arrived on the mountain, did other the Mansi agree to follow.

Судебно-медицинским вскрытием трупов установлено, что смерть Колеватова наступила от действия низкой температуры ( замерз ), Колеватов не имеет телесных повреждений. Смерть Дубининой, Тибо-Бриньоль и Золотарева наступила в результате множественных телесных повреждений. У Дубининой имеется симметричный перелом ребер: справа 2,3,4,5 и слева 2,3,4,5,6,7. Кроме того, обширное кровоизлияние, в сердце.

Тибо-Бриньоль имеет обширное кровоизлияние в правую височную мышцу - соответственно ему - вдавленный перелом костей черепа размером 9х 7 см.с дефектом кости 3 х2 см.

Золотарев имеет перелом ребер справа 2,3,4,5 и 6 по окологрудной и средне-ключичной линии,что и повлекло его смерть.

Физико-технической экспертизой установлено,что одежда Золотарева и особенно Дубининой значительно загрязнена радиоактивной пылью.

Так, остатки брюк Кривонищенко, которыми была завернута нога Дубининой ( в таблице экспертизы пор.№ 60) дает 9.900 полураспадов в минуту со 150 кв.см. , низ от свитра Золотарева ( в таблице экспертизы пор.№ 2 ) дает 5600 полураспадов, что значительно превышает допустимую санитарными правилами,норму загрязненности одежды для лиц, работающих с радиоактивными веществами. Ни Золотарев, ни Дубинина с радиоактивными веществами не работали.

Если принять во внимание,что до обнаружения трупы Золотарева и Дубининой длительное время находились в воде,то следует считать, что радиоактивное заражение их было значительным.

Произведенным расследованием же установлено присутствия I или 2 февраля 1959 г. в районе высоты "1079" других людей, кроме группы туристов Дятлова. Установлено также,что население народности манси, проживавшее в 80-100 км. от этого места, относится к русским дружелюбно, предоставляет туристам ночлег, оказывает им помощь и т.д. Место же гибели группы, в зимнее время считается у манси непригодным для охоты и оленеводства.

Учитывая отсутствие на трупах наружных телесных повреждений и признаков борьбы, наличие всех ценностей группы, а также принимая во внимание заключение судебно-медицинской экспертизы о причинах смерти туристов, следует считать,что причиной гибели туристов явилась стихийная сила, преодолеть которую туристы были не в состоянии.

За недостатки в организации туристской работы и слабый контроль бюро Свердловского ГК КПСС указывалось в партийном порядке: директора Уральского политехнического института Сиунова.

Some suggested that if the Mansi did murder the Dyatlov ski hikers, then they would probably have taken the alcohol from the tent, as well as all the money. But there is the testimony of Ivan Pashin, who said that one of the Mansi who took part in the search refused to drink that alcohol when it was brought back to the rescue camp by Slobtsov and Sharavin. Alexey Cheglakov, another local hunter who helped in the search, also refused to drink that vodka, and not merely out of respect for missing people. The reason for declining was later suggested by his son Vladimir, who said that his father 'respected the Mansi customs, because the place where they found the tent and the dead bodies was a sacred place for the Mansi.' (2) In other words he thought it possible that they were simply afraid to drink alcohol taken from the sacred mountain.

Gennady Karpushin, senior navigational officer in the 123rd Aircraft Division of the Ural Civil Aviation Department, who took part in the search for the group, later told the *Argumenty i Fakty* newspaper:

> In the past, I have flown in those areas, and several times I heard from local hunters about the existence of temples there. The destruction of these temples resulted in death. To this day, I can remember an event that happened on the People's Mountain, which is geographically close to those places. Some geologists had been developing rock crystals (mines) there. Prisoners on a work-release program assisted them in their work. One day, four of these prisoners stole one of these idols. All of them were shot by the Mansi.
>
> And in the area of the Dyatlov pass, there's a small volcanic mountain called Hoy-Ekva. In August 1949, a large surveying operation was conducted from the air, and we noticed a huge gathering of the Mansi on reindeer, who had come there from the surrounding villages. Remembering the stories I heard earlier, I could only suppose one of those temples was there.

Apparently, the Mansi, in seeing these tourists come too close to the holy place, decided to scare them.

The name, Hoi-Ekva, is literally translated as 'Stop, Woman!'. Vladimir Korotaev recalls that, when they received information that the bodies of the students had been discovered, he was summoned to the office of Ivan Prodanov, First Secretary of the Ivdel Communist Party branch, who said:

There was a murder, and the Mansi are the murderers. I witnessed this myself in 1939: a female geologist was found thrown in a lake with her hands and feet tied. This is a sacred place; that is, women are not allowed to be there. In this group, as is known, there were two women: Dubinina and Kolmogorova.

Ethnographers say the sacred place was extremely important for the indigenous people. Ismail Gemuev, an ethnographer and anthropologist, who published several pieces of scientific research on the beliefs of the area, states: 'It was the centre of the Universe in its horizontal dimension.' (3) Gemuev gives numerous examples of how the primary reason for establishing and keeping certain places sacred was 'the clearness' of the ground, the emptiness – which implied that walking on it was forbidden, especially for women. (4)

In the seventeenth century, a sacred place could easily be found not far from any settlement, and all the family members knew the rules of entering it, while strangers had no right to walk there without special permission. But with the growth of settlements, as well as with the appearance of more Russian villages around the Mansi and the Khanty, they began to put their places in more and more remote areas to avoid unwitting trespassing by strangers and animals that would tarnish the pureness of the place.

Even today, all these traditions are still observed. 'We have grounds to think that this tradition, being very sustainable, has preserved itself in general at the present time.' (5)

Alexander Stesin describes the conversation with Roman Anyamov, the local Mansi guide, whom modern ethnographers wanted to hire to take them to the sacred place.

'You can't go there! We get together there and we worship the river.'

He was ready to show me everything, but not a sacred place, because those are what the Mansi must hide from the view of strangers.' (6)

Another member of the search-and-rescue team, Atmanaki, testified for the criminal case record: 'I was with the Bakhtiyarov on 13 February. They refused to take us to the top of the mountain, citing the fact it was a long way in deep snow etc., but they promised to show us the track. They welcomed us more or less politely.'

Hospitality is typical for most people inhabiting northern areas. If somebody enters a home, the host will welcome him and share with him what he has. But this doesn't diminish the distinction between 'them' and 'us'.

After the Stesin group spent several days in the company of this friendly man Roman Anyamov, they met his friend, Untya Pelikoff, a young man in his thirties. He was rather short, as are most Mansi. He came to the settlement of Treskolye after having been drinking for four days.

They had an interesting conversation; even more interesting considering that the fellow was drunk and not mindful of what he was saying.

'Don't look at me like I'm drunk,' said Untya, 'It's better for you to say, what nationality are you?'

'Are you Chinese?' he asked one of the group members. 'Definitely, you are! And this one? Is he a Georgian?'

When he was told the man was a Jew, Untya concluded that Jews were even worse that Chinese. Roman Anyamov tried to stop him talking.

'Untya, say goodbye, the ethnographers are leaving.'

'Well let them go – leave; after you more of the same will come. You all look the same to us.'

'No, ones like this won't come,' said Roma, 'Don't listen to Untya. Sasha, Vlad; ones the same as you won't come, that I can definitely tell you.'

'Don't lie uncle Roma, you don't need to lie. Pack up, go on, bitches, no one loves you here.'

They hugged each other and, staggering, holding one another, went off in the direction of Stepan Anyamov's house. (7)

In fact, there are some grounds for such dislike. On December 4, 2012, the Russian newspaper *Komsomolskaya Pravda* published a story about the Mansi settlement Ushma, a godforsaken place without electricity and with no bus or other connection to the rest of the world. Russians, seeking new opportunities for their businesses, began to visit this settlement in their cars.

As the native people of the taiga, the Mansi have full rights to hunt for valuable fur animals in the taiga, while for Russians this right was strictly limited. So, the Russians were interested in buying fur from the Mansi, and there were some individuals who found a way of obtaining this fur without paying for it. They started bringing low-quality alcohol and devices to watch videos, and pornographic movies, to the settlement.

The peak of this activity was in the 1990s, when Russia was at its most unstable. The article in *Komsomolskaya Pravda* tells the story of a Russian father and a son, who were the most active in supplying the Mansi with alcohol and pornography. The elders of the settlement asked them to stop bringing in these items, since they were corrupting the young people of the settlement. But the two Russians didn't pay any attention to the elders. So, one day on their way to Ushma, the two disappeared, and neither their relatives nor the police ever found them.

Unfortunately, the problem wasn't resolved, and new Russian arrivals continued with the same activities. To resist further intrusion, the locals torched the bridges over the rivers *en route* to Ushma.

This remorseless infringement upon, and interference with, indigenous peoples is now well documented around the globe. Cultural and genetic diversity is rapidly being lost. No one has come up with a long lasting solution. In 300 years, nowhere have tribes been afforded permanent relief from the expectations of the modern world. And in 1959, local tribes sought only one thing from the almighty Russians around them: 'Do not intrude upon our territory.'

Reading national tales and folk stories infuses any reader with the feeling of the times and culture from which they come, reflecting some of the national consciousness: one can feel that the murder of strangers, even be they guests, was quite a real possibility.

Gemuev gives an example in his collection of local folk tales:

> There was one family – father and sons. Three Nenets people came to them all the way from the Kara Sea. The family fed the visitors, and after the guests fell asleep the sons of the old man started to talk to each other. One of the brothers said: 'The Nenets have eaten meat and are asleep. Let's kill them.' The other brother answered: 'No, let us ask father first.' The father told them: 'Don't kill them but let them became our slaves and work for us.' (8)

It is said that furtiveness was originally a part of indigenous people's culture. This may be true, but they had reason – one should not forget the forced baptisms instigated under Peter the Great, and later their forced secularisation under Communist rule. At this time, they had learned to live double lives, to remain closed in unknown company, and this of course merely reflected the general situation of double standards in the Soviet society of the era.

The newer generation of shamans sometimes combined their traditional functions with work for the party system. There were examples when a party functionary was at the same time a practicing shaman. In fact, the ability to speak loudly and confidently was important for both activities! Stepan Kourikov, who took part in the search, was that kind of shaman.

The prosecutor ordered the investigators to find out who of the Mansi were absent from their yurts during the supposed time of the tragedy. Andrei (Alexeevich) Anaymov stated for the criminal case record:

> Around the end of January, beginning of February of 1959 we saw narrow ski tracks while hunting in the woods near the river Auspia. The tracks were obvious in clear places and in the woods they were slightly covered with snow. I was skiing and with me there were three more people: yet another Anyamov Andrei and also my nephew Anaymov Nikolai (Pavlovich) and Tseskin Konstantin. We did not see the Russian tourists. When we were hunting there was good weather in general but some days were bad.

This statement again overturns Lev Ivanov's official conclusion that during winter locals do not hunt in the area. And there are facts that suggest they were hunting not merely in the woods but also on the scene. There was the discovery of a so-called "choom" only 800 m (0.5 mi) from the Dyatlov group's tent. The wording here is simply traditional for the case vocabulary because *choom* means 'house' while the construction discovered had only a symbolic purpose; that is why there are quotation marks.

According to Vladimir Androsov, who lived in the area next to the Mansi all his life, and is very familiar with their traditions and beliefs, the "choom" is a place of sacrifice. The purpose of any blood sacrifice performed by indigenous people was to ask God to protect reindeer from wolves, from diseases, to provide more food for their reindeers, etc. (9) Really, native minorities of Russian North don't perform human sacrifices, and the following quote

This construction is referred to as *choom* and was found meters from the tent.
Photo by one of the searching party members.

from a modern Mansi, Roman Anyamov, repeated as it is written by ethnographers, reflects his intention to impress or scare them. Here he talks of his tribal god sacrifice:

> 'He (GOD) would be brought a sacrificial rooster. And when there wasn't a rooster, it was said, it was necessary to steal a sacrifice, a Russian baby.' Roma looked at us expectantly. 'Well that was a long time ago, and now they don't do that. Barbarism. A rooster is better.' (10)

In the criminal case, the latter part of the statement of Ivan Uvarov, the old man who said the wind could produce some terrible sounds, says:

> About the Mansi, I know that their sacred mountain is about 40 km (24mi) south from the place of the deaths. Forty-five years ago there was one accident with a hunter from the Pershino settlement. He climbed that mountain and took part of the food they had left there for their gods. He

brought some of it back to his home. He did this again but then disappeared and was never seen again. There were some rumours he took an arrow designed for hunting animals.

Another explanation describes the choom as a simple mark of the spot where a moose has been killed. The Mansi routinely leave information about their hunting on trees, as was noticed by Zina who wrote in her diary that there were all kinds of obscure and mysterious signs around. Two antlers of a moose united as a pair indicate that they came from an animal that was killed because it is impossible to find two single horns together, unless it was the season for moose to shed them naturally and, impossibly, they had been separately found and somehow re-united. But significantly, the choom indicates the presence of hunters on the scene.

Some research conducted by one of the rescue group, Valentin Yakimenko, proves that the spot under the cedar (the tree pad with the remains of yet another fire and the snow cave) was most probably where hunters had previously stayed while hunting in the area. This may explain who had made the bed of trees when the students were without knives (with the exception of a small pen knife found in Rustem's breast pocket).

One of the rescue team, then a cadet Khamza Sinyukaev, recalls about tribal people coming out of the woods into the open near the slope as helicopters flew by. These were not those who took part in the rescue operation but others, who Khamza called "the Khanty" or "the Mansi". According to Sinyukaev, they would quickly come on their reindeer to trade golden sand and valuable furs for food, vodka and bullets from the pilots. Therefore, the tribal people were in the area and it didn't take them long to show up at any moment.

Askinadze recalls that it was the Kourikov brothers who finally pointed out the exact place in the ravine in which to dig. 'The Kourikovs discussed something in their language … and went to Ortyukov's tent. Stepan Kourikov told Ortyukov to dig in the area of fir-tree branches.' Looking at the surviving pictures, it looks like a pinpoint excavation of the snow at the indicated spot.

The tree pad discovered under the 2,5 meters of snow looks like a pinpoint excavation

There is an old gentleman, Oleg Shusharin, formerly a keen mountain hiker, who is still alive and who commented on the incident for Federal TV. The year after the tragedy, Oleg led another group of climbers on an expedition in the area. They had just stopped in a small settlement on the way, to replenish their food supply. Some of the group entered the local grocery shop. Oleg himself was waiting outside on the bench.

An old indigenous man was sitting next to him on the bench. 'Was it your fellow students that perished in our mountains a year ago?' he asked suddenly.

When Shusharin affirmed this, the man said with a low voice: 'It was us who killed them.' And he went away. (11)

Dmitry Volkov, who is a popular Russian psychic, was once asked about the cause of death of the Dyatlov group. He said: 'Ask any shaman of the area and he will tell you what happened to them. They entered a territory they were forbidden to enter.'

# 5

But was there sufficient motivation for such violence? Indigenous people are typically simple and gentle. It is hard to explain why they should become enraged immediately upon meeting some complete strangers on their route.

Besides the obvious intrusion of strangers and, even worse, women, upon the sacred territory, it is important to mention that this particular period of time was marked for the Mansi by the loss of a great number of reindeer. Here is the testimony of the Mansi man Petr Bakhtiyarov in the criminal case:

> Every Mansi in the Ural mountains lost about a half of their reindeer herd, because of the disease called *kopytka* [necrobacteriosis].

That year is remembered even by the modern Mansi as the time when 'many reindeer died.' Reindeer herds in the Soviet era were not the property of the Mansi anymore, but 'belonged to the state', as did everything in the country. Eugeny Lysenko, one of the descendants of Bakhtiyarov, living in the Treskolye settlement, said in an interview that his relatives were persecuted by the local authorities who accused them of illegally 'eating or selling the reindeer meat.'

This extreme situation may have inclined to make the hunters 'desperate and culturally exhausted', if not Russian-hating; and one could argue that it might have provoked fears that God's wrath would be even harder on them for allowing a violation of the sacred mountain.

The fireballs in the sky triggered the attack and were perceived by the natives as a clear sign of their god's wrath. But how could they actually kill nine sturdy people who would definitely fight back?

Various peoples of the Russian North are typically small in stature and don't look at all like athletes. And yet, when a small Mansi or Khanty enters the enormous taiga he feels at home there and invariably wins his single combat with the elements. An elderly indigenous woman may live all by herself in a hut in the forest and go hunting for moose, having hunted bear when she was younger. Over the ages these minor peoples were aware that they were relatively few, but they often believed that due to their magical connection with the Spirits, they possessed abilities the Christians lacked. A final triumph over Russians is the leitmotif of many national tales and this idea is always present in their picture of the ideal world, as it is preserved by the old-timers. (12) This becomes obvious from interviews conducted with them by ethnographers and from their folklore as well.

It is a widely known fact that Northern shamans eat mushrooms, known as *Amanita muscaria*, to enter a special trance to communicate with spirits and perform magic rituals. In the Mansi folklore, shamans were even called 'men eating Fly Agaric.' The shaman knows everything about its abilities and they use mushrooms to achieve a special state that ultimately opens their access to 'the Spirits' who then answer their questions and tell them what to do. Often these questions concern the best ways to cure sick people or to find lost people or animals.

There are no clinical trials of fly agaric available for analysis. The chemical composition of it is not constant and has not been studied as well as, say, peyote cactus or mushrooms of the psilocybin type. It depends on the place and conditions where it grows, on the time of picking and the means used for preparing and storage. Its influence on a person also depends on many factors such as the length of his previous experience and the intervals in eating it, as well as the personal traits of his character, psychological background and the cultural context of consumption. (13) That is why a European consumer can be disappointed if trying it. It is important to note that the *Amanita muscaria* that grows in Europe is more toxic than it is in Siberia and thus can bring not only disappointment but death by poisoning, and it is said for the genetic code of a European it is more harmful than it is for an indigenous man of the Russian North. (14)

Here is how the German scientist Johann Georgi described what he observed in 1787 while in his north-eastern geographic expedition among the Ostyak people (the name for modern Khanty). 'Many people of the North practice intoxication by the fly agaric and especially Ostyaks. When someone eats a fresh fly agaric or drinks a concoction of three dried ones, he first becomes very talkative and sings songs, reads poems, jumps and manifests unusual strength.' (15)

The quote above is taken from *Sibirskaya Zaimka*, (2001), a Siberian Scientific journal. The publication states that the mushroom was used not only by shamans but also by ordinary people, though even in Siberia not all species of fly agaric are psychoactive and the right ones could only be found very far into the taiga – which naturally limited their availability. Raised in this mushroom-enjoying culture the hunters knew the difference between the consumption of dry stipes of old specimens and the untwisted and caps of baby fly agaric peeled and taken fresh. The first were capable of provoking the deranged state and hallucinations and thus were to be eaten only by shamans or under the supervision of shamans. The latter, if taken in the right quantity, were a routine way to overcome long distances on snow, to run faster after the reindeer, to hear the silent steps of distant animals and fearlessly to attack even dangerous bears and moose. 'The person's agility increases and physical strength goes above normal. That is why some hunters of dears consume fly agaric before hunting in order to boost their dexterity' states the *Journal of Ethnopharmacology.* (16)

Incredibly, if wounded, hunters under fly agaric did not feel any pain. Ancient national costumes of Northern people had special little bags where they carried a mushroom powder for emergency situations. Some modern consumers of the mushroom (those who were lucky enough to get the right dose and not to end up in an emergency ward) share their experience on Internet forums. One of them testifies that 'after taking the mixture of it with vodka, folks can easily break young birch trees as thick as an arm'.

It was only during the feasts celebrating a successful hunting trip that ordinary people let themselves go further, and ate the old dried specimens. And since not all of these were actually psychoactive and the right ones could be found only deep in the taiga, they had limited availability and not everyone could afford them. Nineteenth-century researches of the Siberian peoples discovered that 'instead of wine they use red mushrooms called Fly Agaric and become drunk or, better to say, utterly wild. Those who have no mushrooms will drink the urine of those who are already frantic, and they become even wilder than the first.' (17)

Ibotenic acid and muscimol are the active components. The two alkaloids of the *Amanita muscaria* – muscarine and mikoatropin – do not break down in the body but are excreted in a dissolved state. This makes the urine as psychotropic as the mushrooms themselves even though it might pass through the bodies of about five people.

In her monograph published by the Russian Academy of Sciences, M. Davlet makes a guess that the Spirits depicted above 'have leather vessels filled with fly agaric tincture attached to their belts.' (18)

The resulting actions depend, to a huge extent, on the individual's personal traits and the cultural context of the consumption of the mushroom. Calm people can just feel thrilled by contemplation of the Universe. Impulsive and nervous people may become aggressive. It is a time when the subconscious impulses rule. (19)

After the Communist revolution the new authorities persecuted shamans and ordinary people for consuming fly agaric. Alcohol became more popular among the ingenious people of North. It was easier to obtain and less dangerous to consume given that even among them, there were cases when someone ate the mushroom and did not come back from his trip, or even went blind. In an expedition to Kamchatka in 1994, I. Zaltsman described one Koryak man who ate a fly agaric and started to sing and then became blind.

Scientists have yet to unravel the mysteries of fly agaric. Alexey Zhirkov, a medical doctor and an ethnic member of the Itelmen (Kamchadal) people, who still practices the shamanic culture of his ancestors, summarizes the quality of it:

One cap can make you work all night with a clear head. Three caps can make you feel high. And ten caps provoke hallucinations. All your senses become sharp. You can hear water drops falling somewhere five miles away. You don't feel pain. Truth be told that there is no sex under fly agaric. But you are capable of doing any kind of work tirelessly. (20)

# PART VI: A SOLUTION TO THE DYATLOV PASS MYSTERY

# 1

It is quite obvious that the very first suspects, the Mansi, at least knew who killed the Dyatlov team and, most likely, silently approved. When interrogated, they drew strange round and oval orbits for investigator Korotaev. These drawings later disappeared from the criminal case files but they definitely represented the fireballs which the hunters interpreted as theirs gods' wrath against the intruders.

The reason why the tent was attacked is partly explained above and partly can be inferred from the testimony of Igor Gorbushin, the local policeman:

> At the very beginning of March, I was at the local police station talking to some people about the accident where the hikers had died. A Mansi man approached us. I don't know his name, but I have since been informed he was called Kourikov. He was asked how these students could have died. He said, next to the sacred mountain (but he didn't mention exactly where), live five Ostyak people. The Ostyak are a kind of wild people and are not friends with the Mansi or with the Russians. They never come to Ivdel. These people could have killed the tourists, **because they came too close to their sacred mountain**, or maybe **they thought the tourists were hunting their deer or moose**.
>
> Kourikov said it was only conjecture and he didn't really know. But he said he'd seen these Ostyaks several years ago, though he didn't know which mountain was their sacred one.

The Ostyak, again, are indigenous people calling themselves Khanty and living in *Khanty of the Mansi*, an autonomous region of Russia situated pretty far from the Dyatlov Pass. Grigory Kourikov, the shaman, refuted any of the claims made by Gorbushin. In this case we deal with contradictory statements - one made by a policemen and the other by the interrogated person. It may be that the policeman talked to some other Kourikov, because many of the Mansi shared the same last name, or for some reasons Kourikov didn't want his private statement to be registered by the investigation.

In any case, chances are that the Mansi knew about the tragedy before anyone else did. The following document is a secret order sent by the regional prosecutor to Major Bizyaev, the police chief of Ivdel:

> In addition to the current tasks in regards to the death of the hikers of the Dyatlov group, please check the following: Makrushin, the chairman of the Burmansk village council, is spreading rumours that, supposedly, the Mansi Pavel Grigorievich Bakhtiyarov **saw how the hikers fell from the mountain,** and told other Mansi persons about this on 17 February, 1959.

There is an interesting enquiry made on March 12, reported by Frol Zietsov, who worked in the settlement.

> On 2 March in the guest house of another expedition, I saw two Mansi dressed not like the Mansi, but like Russians, just in their coats. One of them started writing and he put his note in an envelope, which he passed to the other.

Looking over his shoulder, I saw the last name of Kourikov while he was writing.

Considering there weren't many Mansi families in the area, the claim that Zhiltsov saw some 'unknown Mansi' sounds rather strange. Might this suggest there were people staying in the area whom he'd never seen before?

Moreover, the unknown Mansi he saw were dressed the way everyone dressed in the town. They didn't want to be noticed. Their silent communication is also interesting: one wrote something on a piece of paper and gave it to the other.

### A reconstruction of what I believe really happened on the mountain

Natalia Sakharova, a retired police colonel with 25 years of service, was an expert in a police department in one of the most criminal districts of Irkutsk. She also has additional education as a medical doctor and currently works at the Criminal Expert Bureau. Having scrutinized the full Criminal Case on the Dyatlov group, she came to the conclusion that what happened in 1959 on the slope of Kholat Syakhl Mountain was murder. I have already cited her opinion on how the investigation failed to prove that the tent was cut from inside.

According to Sakharova:

We can make certain assumptions based on the analysis of the photos of the tent we have. The area around the tent was intentionally covered with snow in order to disguise possible prints (those of footwear, a fight, dragging, and the real method of exit from the tent).

With the way the snow was covering the tent it was not possible to perform linear cuts in the side because it had to be straightened. So the cuts were performed before the snow was brought there. It seems that the actions had the following consequence: first, the standing tent was cut...

The cuts of the tent appear to be made with two different knives (photos below). The first one was rather blunt because it left fringe and even didn't cut some of the threads. The second one was made with a very sharp blade. It easily went through the seam area and left the edges looking even. There were three Finnish knives that belonged to the students. Tibo and Krivonischenko's knives were found in their taurpalin's pockets (CC, Vol 2, p.41) ("taurpalin" is a wind proof jacket) which would imply that the knives were not used at the very moment of the attack. In fact, we still don't know with which knife the tent was cut and whether it really was cut from inside. Yuri Kuntsevich, the head of the Dyatlov foundation in Ekaterinburg, said he still doesn't exclude the possibility that the tent had been cut from outside. According to him, it very well could be that somebody first pierced the tent's material and than turned the blade of his knife and ripped the fabric through making it look like if it was done from inside.

Vladislav Karelin stated to the investigation that it would have taken at least ten armed men to scare the Dyatlov group. He later said that it was Lev Ivanov who imposed this statement to him because Ivanov's initial version was the attack of armed people. It looks like the gunmen whoever they were forced some of the students to take off their footwear. There was a pretty strange pile of *valenki* right in the centre of the tent. It's as if the attackers just picked them up off of the ground and threw them back in the tent. Maslennikov stated that there were three pairs of *valenki* and one single one in the middle of the tent. Rustem Slobodin was wearing the missing *valenki*. Igor Dyatlov's slippers were found outside the tent. Captain Chernyshov stated: 'About 10-15 m (32-49 ft) from the tent we saw slippers and Dyatlov's fur jacket. Also we saw a tarpaulin (windproof jacket).'

Forensic pathologists have frequently described people who in the last stages of hypothermia throw off their clothes partially or completely, regardless of the presence or absence of alcohol in their blood. Coroners have frequently found cases of undressing 'on the go,' when items of clothing are scattered along the path of a person who is freezing. It also happens that a person may undress in one place, and the clothes are then scattered around the corpse or may even lie beneath it. However, it is unlikely that Dyatlov and his fellow group members would undress themselves right next to the tent when their state was still far from the terminal stage of freezing. It is as though someone made them take their clothes off as well as their footwear.

Why wouldn't they have tried to fight back? They most likely did try, judging by the state of their fists and faces. Besides, the area next to the tent was not examined properly, and most likely was hid under the snow brought there to cover the prints, according to Sakharova. That is why there were no prints right around the tent, but they were very well preserved to the side (according to Koptelov and Sharavin who both testify that the footprints were visible at a distance of approximately 7-10 metres, or 22-32 ft). It might also be that at a certain moment Dyatlov decided that it would be wiser for the group to step back and not to further antagonise the armed interlopers.

The students were forced to stand in one line. Yuri Kopte-lov, the rescue team member who found the first two bodies, recently made a drawing of the footprints nearest to the tent as they appeared to him and Sharavin. It seemed that the people were not walking but **standing** in one row, shoulder to shoulder. Anyone can tell the difference between the footprints of a standing person from those of someone walking. Then, perhaps, the attackers forced them at gunpoint to leave the sacred territory, which led to their deaths from hypothermia.

Slobtsov's statement, taken from the criminal case file, is as follows:

> The footprints were not proceeding in single file, but were abreast in a horizontal line, sometimes closer and converging, sometimes not.
>
> I had the feeling the hikers had left the tent in an organized state. It also seems that they were scared, possibly even holding each other by the hand in the darkness.

Captain Chernyshov states in his testimony for the criminal case: 'For about thirty or forty metres I saw very good human footprints walking abreast in parallel chains, as if they were holding each other.'

This suggests something more along the lines of the hikers having been forced out of the area at gunpoint, as opposed to the theory that has them running around in different directions panicked by some infrasound they could not deal with.

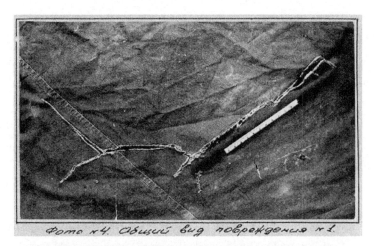

Фото № 4. Общий вид повреждения № 1.

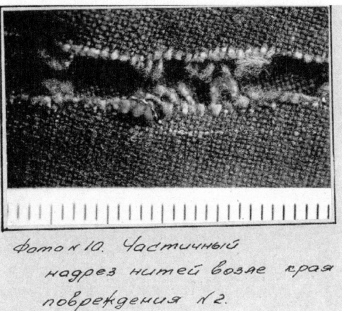

Фото № 10. Частичный надрез нитей возле края повреждения № 2.

(1) The cut is made with a very sharp knife. It easily went through the seam area and left the edges of the cut looking even. The cut (2) is made with a different blade

199

The attackers could then have entered the tent and searched it. It does look like a search of sorts was conducted, as evidenced by the disrupted state of things strewn about. Sakharova assumed the tent was checked inside with the flashlight which was found on the snow, then the whole tent was covered with snow, which caused sagging. Then the flash light was placed upon it. (21) To prevent the students from returning, they then cut the tent to render it unusable.

There was a very strange curved cut (1) right next to the entrance. It definitely was not used to escape from the tent (there were no attempts to tear the tent here). It was also made by another type of blade, which was much sharper than the one that made the upper cut (2).

The results of the expert analysis show that in addition to the sides that were slashed there were some smaller, seemingly random cuts and punctures. The scored ski pole with its upper part cut may have been used to hold up the ridge of the tent; or perhaps it can simply be linked to a general intent to destroy.

Having been marched off the mountain, every student acted according to his or her mental and physical strength. A good example is what happened to Lyudmila Korovina's group in the Kharan-Darban Mountains in 1993. There were seven people who ranged in age from 17 to 19 years old. Rain fell for a few days, and the members of the group were freezing and tired. They also pitched the tent on a slope for a night in an uncomfortable spot. In the morning, the strongest and oldest of the group, a 24-year-old named Alexander, suddenly collapsed and died. It is possible that he was struck by altitude sickness. Korovina, the leader of the group, told everyone to go to the forest, and she was left alone with the corpse. The group started to descend but then for some reason they returned. Upon their return, they realized that Korovina had also died. In reality, she was still alive, but unconscious. They started to panic, scream, run around, tear off their clothes, and beat themselves against rocks. Only one girl, Valentina Utochenko, managed to maintain her self-control and tell the story of this terrible tragedy. In the end, Utochenko left them and went to the forest herself. She slept there all night in a sleeping bag and returned to the slope in the morning. All of the members of the group were dead. They lay in different directions, but all within sight of each other.

During panic causing events, there is always at least one person with stronger nerves who is not affected. Dyatlov's group were hardened and experienced but still they were very young and found themselves in a much worse situation. That is why I don't agree with the formal explanation why Doroshenko and Krivonischenko died next to the cedar. Their actions at this point could have been affected by their mental and physical state. It might also very well be that they climbed the cedar to observe what was going on near the tent. Krivonischenko might have frozen up there and fallen down, because branches of the cedar were found under his body. The drop itself could have rendered him unconscious, and subsequently he soon died of exposure. Doroshenko might have been affected by the sight of his friend's death and it broke his determination to survive. He was found with his face covered with grey foam, which could also be the result of pulmonary edema. Had he been in his senses he certainly would have wiped his face with his sleeve.

So probably when the attackers later came to check the situation the two Yuris were already dead. The hunters could have checked whether or not Doroshenko was still alive by pressing a burning ember to his leg, which caused the leg burn of 31 x 10 cm. (12 x 3"). It might be that no one actually undressed the corpses of Krivonischenko and Doroshenko in order to warm themselves, especially since the clothes were found scattered on the bed of trees in the ravine. There is no evidence that the clothes were used by other members of the group. However, Dyatlov was wearing a vest originally worn by Doroshenko.

I believe that Slobodin and Zina were unconscious for some time after the blunt blows they received to their heads, but later (perhaps even after the attackers had gone) they came to and tried to crawl back to the tent and died in the process.

According to Sakharova, the group had become divided either due to coercion (it is harder to survive in such harsh conditions while separated) or because they were hiding from the attackers.

It could be that Zolotariov and Tibo were not in the tent at the moment of the attack and were brought to the group by the attackers. The last four were killed next to the cedar and taken to the ravine to hide their terrible injuries (their livor mortis does not match their bodies' positions). All of them were searched – the pockets unbuttoned. (23)

My opinion, however, is that the last four were hiding in the ravine. They most likely tried to escape, and that is why their bodies were found aside of the tree pad.

As was mentioned earlier, low temperatures can lengthen the time for the formation of livor mortis; and as the livor mortis was already present, the bodies were turned and checked not earlier than one day after the tragedy. Also, searching the pockets would have been reasonable in daylight. Who else had the opportunity to come to the scene again except for those who were in the area?

The following is merely speculation which I in no way claim to be correct. We know that some of the clothes where spoiled and this could be explained by attempts to cut them from their dead bodies. Yet it is also a part of certain aboriginal beliefs (of the Khanty) that it is necessary to destroy the personal effects of the dead, including their clothes, in order not to help the souls of the dead should they come back to earth again. Death is perceived as a kind of fainting: immediately after the death, the person doesn't know anything, but a day later they recover consciousness and can recognize people. It is only when they see signs (cuts) on their clothes that they realize they are dead. They have no choice but to go to the place of the dead. (24)

## The most puzzling injuries and a missing tongue

We don't know exactly if the mushrooms were involved but it seems quite possible that the experienced hunters used them in order to be strong and wild enough to attack bears and moose in the harsh conditions of the Ural Mountains during winter. According to the reputed researcher of the Russian North, S. Krasheninnikov, who lived with the Koryak people for some time in the 19th century, they would also eat fly agaric when they intended to kill someone. (22)

Dubinina had her number 2, 3, 4, and 5 ribs broken on the right side and number 2, 3, 4, 5, 6, and 7 ribs on the left side. Zolotariov had a flail chest (a detachment of part of the rib wall) with broken 2, 3, 4, 5 and 6 ribs on the right side. There was speculation that the rib fractures might have been caused by unskilled resuscitation as the others tried to perform CPR on Lyuda. However, it was realised that in this case, pneumothorax and fractures would have appeared as the result of repeated action associated with CPR.

In any case, histological (tissue-related) tests were performed on the bodies found in May and, on the basis of the state of the bone fragments it was suggested the bodies suffered a one-time impact. Indeed, since the histological analysis of Zolotariov showed bone fragments, perhaps Zolotariov suffered two strikes. The histological examination also discovered inner haemorrhaging for both people, which confirms the ribs were broken while they were still alive. It sounds horribly certain that someone jumped on their rib cages.

Those who believe that a loud sound followed by panic caused the group to break out of the tent, still cannot answer the question of who or what finally managed to break so many ribs in one blow without leaving any bruising. And if this occurred from falling into a ravine, why did no one have a broken leg or wrist, which usually happens first?

A compression injury could be a good explanation, such as a hug from a bear or a large amount of soft snow as is found in an avalanche. But, as already mentioned, there should be additional indications of the impact. For instance, with an avalanche, these indications might be signs of asphyxia or suffocation, such as small haemorrhaging on the conjunctiva, or a shield of ice around the nose and mouth. Again, if there had been just a limited impact from a layer of snow, that is, the 'snow slab', then compressed trauma of the rib cage would have caused rib fractures first along the midaxillary line (that is, on the side), and only then the fracture of the ribs on the back (because the flexibility of the ribs on the back side of the rib cage is much less than it is on the frontal side). Only if the compression was much stronger would the ribs finally have been broken on the frontal part. What we see with Zolotariov is the opposite: there were no rib fractures found on the back side. And this is where Dubinina's ribs were broken.

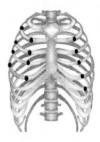

Dubinina's chest damage. He ribs number 2, 3, 4, 5 broken on the right side (both on the frontal and midaxillary lines) and 2, 3, 4, 5, 6, and 7 ribs on the left side

Sometimes, and it is the case with children and young people, if the broadside of an object hits the right anterior-lateral surface of the chest tangentially, fractures can be formed not only in the place of impact, but also in parallel on the opposite side of the chest, as it was with Lyuda. These are called structural fractures.

According to a modern expert commenting on the bodies, Professor Yuri Morozov, a forensic medical examiner with 38 years' experience, their injuries were an isolated incident and were caused by a single impact. Morozov said he was particularly surprised to see the fracture of the second rib. The second rib is under the collarbone and isn't easy to break. From this, it can be assumed something very heavy fell on the body. The ribs of young people are quite resilient. They bend on impact, and it's only possible to break them with a very strong impact force. Morozov suggested that somebody bounced on their chests when they were lying on the snow. So because the impactor's surface was broad, and both Luda and Zolotariov were well dressed and lying on a relatively soft surface such as snow-covered ground, they had no bruising. Dubinina had only one local haematoma, at the right edge of the sternum. (25)

Vigorous bouncing is a plausible explanation. It was observed by the researchers that under the influence of fly agaric, people tend to jump and are capable of jumping to a height as tall as themselves.

My suggestion just a bit different from Sakharova's opinion:

After reviewing the trauma of the last four I can guess that the murderers were professionals. The ribs fractures were specific – they could have been the result of jumping on the victim's chest. The skull injuries can't be the result of falling upon rocks.

Tibo had multiple fractures to the temporal bone (forehead), with extensions to the frontal and sphenoid bones. The shape of the fracture suggested a small impactor with a round surface, such as a club or a blackjack. The coroner (Vozrozhdenny) also stated that this kind of trauma could have occurred if he had been vigorously thrown and fallen and hit against rocks, ice, etc., by a gust of strong wind. Since there was no really strong wind this explanation is not plausible. But he could have been literally thrown by a person. On the Internet forum where modern fly agaric consumers discussed their relevant experiences, one of them testified that he and his friends had thrown some iron gates several meters while setting up a game of football.

But considering the absence of any additional injuries typical of falling, I would rather explain it as a forceful blow, either in the form of a stone or the fist of a person invigorated by the drug taking mentioned. Of course, any impact of this kind would have resulted in the injury of soft tissues unless his head was very well protected, which it was. The coroner describes the head covered by a tightly tied green woollen sports cap and a khaki canvas fur helmet with a zip fastener (like a flying helmet). That is why the soft tissue avoided damage but the bone did not.

Alexander Kolevatov had a bad injury behind his right ear which looked like it was inflicted by a hard object like a gun.

One thing that is not clear is how Igor Dyatlov acted at that time because he is the only one who actually finally died of hypothermia, according to yet another coroner Eduard Tumanov. It appears that he had been tied at the ankle with rope, Tumanov suggested. He was found 300 metres or almost 1000 feet from the cedar and his arms were in a position suggesting they had also been tied. Perhaps it was done in order to limit his movement and get him to freeze. His lips were covered in clotted blood, and his stomach 'contained about 100 cubic cm of a liquid mucosal mass of brown-red colour.' It appears that before he died he was vomiting blood. It may well have been due to the severe stress he endured. (26) No histology or chemical test results exist in the criminal case to state with certainty what may have caused his death.

The final question that has to be answered is: why was one of the group member's tongue missing? Opinions differ regarding the cause of the disturbing absence of Lyuda Dubinina's tongue.

Some say the tongue was eaten by rodents; others argue it was torn or cut out.

Vozrozhdenny himself offered a possible explanation when he wrote in his autopsy report:

> [There is] damage to the soft tissue of the head, and 'bath skin' wrinkling to the extremities are the post-mortem changes (rot and decay) of Ms. Dubinina's corpse, which was under water before it was found.

One might assume that 'soft tissue of the head' also means tongue.

Every autopsy transcript includes a description of the external and internal parts of the body. The missing tongue was already obvious during the external examination. While the autopsy was performed, the coroner also found several other strange things, which were impossible to observe before cutting the throat open. These were

1. The diaphragm of the mouth and tongue was absent.
2. The upper edge of the sublingual bone was bared.

The diaphragm of the mouth is mostly a mylohyoid muscle. It depresses the mandible and elevates the sublingual bone (hyoid), the floor of the oral cavity, and the tongue. It is attached to the hyoid. The coroner Vozrozhdenny saw that the sublingual bone was bared and the mylohyoid muscle was missing only after he performed his internal examination. This assumes that the skin on the throat was intact and no inner injuries were seen: 'The neck is long and thin. The soft tissue in the neck area is flaccid when palpated.'

This raises two questions. How could the mylohyoid muscle, which adjoins so closely to the skin, decay completely while the skin was not damaged? Tissue cannot rot selectively.

Another possibility is that rodents ate it along with the tongue, but in this case, again, their teeth would have damaged the skin. In addition, traces of rodent teeth are very specific, and Vozrozhdenny would have easily recognized them. But he only wrote that 'the tongue in the oral cavity is absent,' and 'the diaphragm of the mouth is absent.' It isn't possible to clarify any of his statements, as he never gave an interview about the autopsy for the rest of his life.

It appears likely that someone used a knife to perform the amputation. However, if this is indeed so, it definitely occurred post-mortem, otherwise there would have been profound bleeding. According to Henrietta Churkin, a forensic pathologist present at the autopsy: 'When it was discovered that Dubinina had no tongue, we wondered even more. I asked Boris [Vozrozhdenny]: "Where could [the tongue] go?" He shrugged his shoulders. It seemed to me he was depressed and even scared.'

# 2

In January 2016 investigator Oleg Vasnin of the Novolyalinsky Police department of Sverdlovsk region was trying to track down the owner of a TOZ-34 gun which emerged recently in one crime. He managed to find a Russian, 72-year-old Anatoly Stepochkin, who owned the gun back in 1981.

The investigator visited the elderly hunter, who lives in Verkhoturye, and while talking to him discovered that it had been given to Stepochkin by a Khanty hunter whose name he couldn't recall. The incident took place in 1981, close to Nyaksimvol, a settlement on the Sosva River. Not far from the river, they had discovered a tent, and in the tent there was a Khanty hunter of about 45 years of age. He had a stove there, and two dogs. The meat of a moose was stored outside the tent. They drank Stolichaya vodka together and started to talk. Stepochkin asked why the Khanty left the meat unattended outside. What if it were to be stolen? The Khanty told him there is no way that anyone could steal anything from him without him finding out who it was and punishing the culprit. 'We are the Masters of this place. We find anyone and punish them for a thing like that,' he said. And he told him a story.

We had a sacred pit where we stored gold and valuable furs. Tourists found that place and they took stuff from there. We found out pretty fast and we started to watch them. At night, we approached the tent. Then our shamans made in a teargas agent [a kind of datura was ignited creating smoke, and in effect, used as a teargas agent to flush or "smoke out" the subjects]. We waited for some time until the tourists started to feel bad and came running out of the tent. Eventually, we finished them all off. (27)

Stepochkin had no idea of the Dyatlov Pass incident at that time because it was not covered in the media until the mid-1990s. He only heard of it about three years ago. Russian people rarely go to the police unless they really need to. They are just afraid of doing so.

Personally I don't believe that the Dyatlov group could find the sacred pit and rob it. There was a so-called Ushma Cave on the group route and they happened to be next to it on the 26th or 27th. It was not far from the 41 Kvartal settlement. They arrived there on the night of the 26th and the next day was their first day walking along the Lozva River via the Ushma settlement. It is then that they were given a sledge so that they would not have to carry their heavy backpacks. Women were strictly forbidden to come within

One of the shots from the hikers' camera with possible entrance to the cave

two kilometres of the cave. According to *Sacred Places of the Ural Mountains and Forests*, women could not even look in the direction of it.

Most likely the attack by the indigenous people was an act of intimidation to discourage other tourists from going in the remote areas. Interestingly, Mikhail Serdyuk, who represents the Khanty-Mansi federal subject in the Russian Parliament doesn't exclude such a possibility, or the involvement of toxic substances. (28)

But if the indigenous people killed everyone, then why were some of the clothes of the victims contaminated with radioactivity? Krivonischenko, whose clothing samples showed the highest degree of contamination not only worked with radioactive substances but was also part of the relief effort crew post the 1957 Kyshtym nuclear disaster. During that time period, it was typical to own only a few clothing items, which were worn for many years.

Yet another possible explanation can be found in the diaries. Lyuda wrote: 'After breakfast, some of the lads, headed by Yuri Yudin, our well-known geologist, went to look for local minerals. They didn't find anything except pyrite and quartz veins in the rock.'

Pyrite is a mineral regularly found in the Urals. But it isn't only pyrite, gold and silver that are found in these mountains. There is also uranium ore, which gives off radioactivity, and which most likely fouled the hikers' trousers and sweaters with radioactive dust. In the notebooks of journalist Grygoriev, who took part in the rescue operation, there is the following entry:

All the backpacks have bits and pieces of rocks … Vishnevsky told me that they were for striking fire in case their matches got damp. I disagreed because I saw that they were rocks taken from the 2nd Severny camp.

It was noticeable to many that the bodies had an unusual skin colour like brick red or brown which was interpreted as the result of chemical (or radioactive) poisoning.

Prior to defrosting, the skin of any corpse will generally preserve its natural or red colour. Yudin recalls the colour of Slobodin's face, when his body was still frozen: it was just 'like anyone else.' According to Morozov a red skin colour is typical in those who have frozen to death.

After defrosting, the face of a dead person is usually hard to recognize. Experts have described these metamorphoses in detail. The wide variety of colour shades of defrosted skin is related to the complex chemical process of blood decay. The arterial blood of a live human being is vividly scarlet, and the venous blood is dark wine-coloured. Decay arises during the conversion of haemoglobin into the chemical compounds haemosiderin, haematoporphyrin and a dozen others. Each of these composites has its own distinct colour. So, when Yudin saw Dyatlov's unfrozen body, he was struck by the dark brown complexion.

However, when he found the still-frozen corpses of Doroshenko and Krivonischenko under the cedars, Yuri Koptelov noticed their complexion was brick coloured. The rescue team members sometimes give different accounts of what they saw. For instance, Sharavin stated repeatedly that he saw a dark blanket on the scene, but Koptelov didn't recall any blankets. Anyway, let's keep in mind that when Koptelov inspected the bodies, he was looking at corpses that had been affected by the weather and UF rays for about a month.

For those who served the Spirits of the Mountain and who guarded it, nothing was remotely as valuable as guarding that Spirit, not even the alcohol and money of those whom the guardians saw as deserving punishment. This would explain why, if the killers had indeed struck, they left without taking anything from their victims.

# 3

The interrogations of the Mansi were formal and very superficial, with some inconsistencies in the individual testimonies. Some denied they had a sacred place at all, some claimed there was such a place where Russians were welcome to go, and some stated they didn't know where it was. They also denied that the mountain where the Dyatlov team died was a sacred mountain, but they probably lied to deflect suspicion from themselves.

Mansi statements indicate that they did in fact meet with different tourist groups that were hiking in the Urals at the same period of time. The testimonies mention groups with seven, ten, or twelve people. It is important to mention that the Dyatlov group was the only one which declared a route toward Otorten.

In Dyatlov's time a number of Mansi settlements, such as Suyevat Paul, consisted of several gers (yurts or nomadic tents) of the Kourikov family. The Bakhtiyarova Jurt, Khandybina Jurt, and Anyamova-Jurt were other settlements in the area, each name before the Jurt indicating families with the same surname lived in the settlement. Mansi Nikolay Bakhtiyarov told the investigator that at the end of the January there was a group of students (8 people, including one or two women) who stayed overnight at his brother Petr Bakhtiyarov's yurt. "In the yurt we talked to these tourists. They said that they are going to the mountains but didn't specify which one exactly. They only asked which way is better to go – on the river or some other and they went along the road toward the river, peak Vels..." By now we know that these students were not the Dyatlov group but another group of students from the city of Rostov who headed to Vels peak. Igor Fomenko led this group (and by coincidence was my literature professor years later at Tver State University). He confirmed his mountaineering party stayed with Petr Bakhtiyarov's family. Comparing his recollections with the statements of the individual Mansi witnesses in the criminal case provided food for thought. Several of Bakhtiyarovs (Nikolai, Nikita, Prokopy) mention that Petr Bakhtyarov did not go hunting at that period of time because he was very sick with tuberculosis. Fomenko also recalled that when his group first arrived at Petr's yurt the owner was away on a hunting trip. When Petr finally arrived home he looked perfectly healthy to Fomenko.

The investigators visited the yurts twice to conduct interrogations but found none of the men there. All, including the allegedly tuberculosis-stricken Petr, were said to be away in the woods looking for their reindeer. Most likely they didn't want to be involved with the investigation. We have already mentioned earlier that Ivan Pashin, a local hunting guide of Russian origin, was similarly reluctant. Pashin "respected the traditions of the Mansi" and refused to approach the tent when it was first discovered and refused to drink the alcohol found in the tent. Except for the Kourikov brothers, most of the Mansi similarly refused to participate in the rescue operation despite offers of good money.

It is pretty natural to assume that had the students met with any of the tribal people, the diary entries certainly would have noted such a meeting. Rustem's, Lyuda's, and Zina's diaries included some basic Mansi vocabulary, consisting of random words: a stone, a brook, a fireplace, a knife, a reindeer, vodka, fish, etc. The most puzzling thing was Zina's deciphering of the tree signs, which originally contained no dates or names. The page on the right contains the Anyamov family's tribal sign, the initials of their family hunters, as well as the date of a hunt, which was a success:

October 5, 1958. Who explained it to her? Who gave her the date? Why did she write it down? (The drawing, which looks like a missile, is indeed a sign of a moose.)

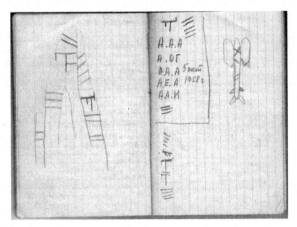

The penultimate page of Zina's diary is a deciphering of Mansi's tree signs

The idea of the possible encounter is supported by some contemporary interviews, like the one with Khamza Sinyukaev, a cadet who took part in the rescue operation. He stressed several times hunters would come to the search party camp each time the helicopters engines were heard in the air and tell the rescue team of their warnings to the perished: "We told them not to go there." (29)

On March 5th, 2018 the First Channel of Russian TV presented a new witness, Beniamin Berenholtz, currently residing in Israel. Berenholtz was said to be the very last person to meet the Dyatlov group. The full version of the show can be accesses at www.youtube.com/watch?v=dN7LSVjpPGs

Berenholtz claimed that back in 1959 while serving his two-year conscription term at the military division 6602 in Kotlia (also known as *Settlement 70*) he met with the Dyatlov group. No indication that the group actually stayed there can be found in the diaries but there is certain toponymic confusion that shrouds their route. For instance, there were two locations both known as Settlement 41. According Berenholtz, he offered the students to use his division's horse and walked with them 18 kilometers (11 miles) up to the place called (Andrew) Anyamova-Jurt. There he left them, as he recalls, on February the 2nd. Berenholtz was of opinion that the students were killed by indigenous people. He didn't claim that Anyamov killed them but mentioned that "the natives had their own secret way to communicate and Anyamov could pass on the information that the group is on its way."

One of Andrew Anyamov's descendants, Valery Anyamov, refuted Berenholtz' allegations as groundless and pointed out the inconsistency in his opponent's distances estimations. However, when both were tried on polygraph, Berenholtz' answers turned out to be true while Valery's statement that he doesn't believe his fellow tribe men could be involved in the crime were found false.

But if the indigenous people were responsible, why keep that a secret? We have already mentioned the general reasons: the whole event was not clear for the authorities and since Ivanov reported pretty strange things like fireballs the decision was taken by the local Party leaders to make the case secret. What is certain is that the KGB – the Soviet state security agency – was present on the mountain during the searches for the bodies. The KGB wanted to make sure, in effect, that members of the Dyatlov team who had access to government secrets, particularly Kolevatov, really were dead, and hadn't escaped abroad. Boris Slobtsov confirmed this, citing the words of Kirilenko, the regional Party leader, who said to the rescue team when they were about to stop the search in May

1959: 'Dig and make sure you find the bodies. Who knows: maybe they decided to fly away to Norway from here!'

Also, the situation in Yekaterinburg when the Dyatlov team died was an unusual one. The women's Distance Skating world championship had just started, which meant this 'closed' city was full of international visitors as it had never been before. The rumours of flying objects and secret weapons tests were on the lips of many people. The government didn't want these rumours to be spread. In the USSR everything was supposed to be good. Planes weren't supposed to crash, crimes weren't supposed to be committed, and no one in a country with such a strong atheistic materialistic ideology was supposed to have ever heard of such madness as hate killings based on heathen beliefs.

When all is said and done, the theories that the nine students camping on the mountainside were killed by some sinister military intervention are very far-fetched, though not as far-fetched as some of the other theories, which vary from science fiction to being simply absurd. There seems to be something in the human mind which enjoys piecing together improbable conspiracy theories. My own belief, that some murderous Khanty were most likely responsible, is not in any way intended to cast aspersions generally on those excellent people; even the best nations have some rogue members. I believe that it is simply the most logical explanation, given the evidence.

In the absence of evidence which Moscow regarded as conclusively implicating the Mansi, it's more likely Moscow simply decided that to blame the indigenous people would indeed be incorrect in the context of the multicultural policy of the USSR. The state was made up of different nations – sometimes against the will of these nations – and for the authorities to admit racism or that these nations didn't get along well would be tantamount to questioning the whole social policy of the Soviet Union.

Moreover, it's a fact that groups of hikers were banned from taking the route toward Otorten for the next four years. The guardians of the sacred area received exactly what they wanted: the exclusive occupation of their territory. And now the state itself was protecting their exclusivity.

This, I think, is a solution to the mystery of Dyatlov Pass. But I say *a* solution, not *the* solution, for in the absence of any completely decisive new evidence, it's impossible and illogical to claim certainty, or to be dogmatic, about what happened. But yes, I do believe that the most likely explanation, based on the evidence which is available, is the one I suggest: that some members of the aboriginal people were responsible.

And if you don't share my conclusion?

After all, you don't need to. What I'm suggesting is only speculative. There is no absolute and decisive evidence for my theory. But I do believe, after sifting carefully through the evidence and studying everything relating to the Dyatlov Pass tragedy and thinking about it, that the theory I'm offering is the most plausible.

And if indeed you don't go along with my theory, then all that can be said is that the mystery of Dyatlov Pass still dwells there, silent, frigid, unyielding, perhaps to remain an enigma for eternity, ghostly and ghastly on the mountainside, held in frozen secrecy by the ice, the snow, and by the howling wind.

And the mountain herself? She offers no explanation beyond a plain, stark warning, embodied in her name:

'Don't go there.'

THE END

# Bibliography for Chapters IV -VI

(1)Varsegov, N. (2014, January 22) Rassledovanie gibeli gruppy Dyatlova bylo nedostovernym. *Komsomolskaya Pravda.* Retrieved from http://www.kp.ru/daily/26184/3073188/

(2) Piscareva M. (2013)Vizzhaitsy o vremeni i o sebe" *Samizdat,* Retrieved from http://samlib.ru/p/piskarewa_m_l/vizhay.shtml

(3)Gemuev I. N. (2000) . Narod Mansi. Voploschenie mifa. Russian Academy of Sciences, Inst. of archeology and ethnography, 33

(4) Ibid., 35

(5) Ibid., 33

(6) Stesin, A. (2008, October1)Lesnye Lyudi. *Journalny Zal.* Retrieved from  http://magazines.russ.ru/october/2008/1/ct11.html

(7) Gemuev, 17

(8) Stesin, A. (2008, October1)Lesnye Lyudi. *Journalny Zal.* Retrieved from  http://magazines.russ.ru/october/2008/1/ct11.html

(9) Piscareva M. (2013)Vizzhaitsy o vremeni i o sebe. *Samizdat.* Retrieved from http://samlib.ru/p/piskarewa_m_l/vizhay.shtml

(10) Stesin, A. (2008, October1)Lesnye Lyudi. *Journalny Zal.* Retrieved from  http://magazines.russ.ru/october/2008/1/ct11.html

(11)Shusharin, O. (Speaker). (2013) Pereval Dyatlova: ne khodi tuda [Television series episode] In Pervy Kanal (Producer), *Pust Govorya*t. Retrieved from http://www.1tv.ru/videoarchive/61020 27:30

(12) Kulemzin, V.M. (2004) O Khantyiskikh Shamanakh. *Tartu*, 156

(13) Dixon, O. (2008) The Mystery of Fly Agaric. N.p.: *Veligor*, 9

(14) Saar, M. (1991) Fungi in Khanty Folk Medicine. *Ethnopharmacol.* V 31: 175-179.

(15) Shapovalov, A. (2001) Magicheski grib mukhomor: k voprosu ob ispolzovanii gribov v shamanskoi praktike. *Sibirskaya Zaimka. History of Siberia in Scientific Publications.* Retrieved from http://zaimka.ru/shapovalov-shaman-amanita/

(16) Saar, M. (1991)Ethnomycological data from Siberia and North-East Asia on the effect of Amanita muscaria. *Ethnopharmacol.* V.31.157-173.

(17) Krasheninnikov, S. (1949) Opisanie zemli Kamchatki. *Glavsevmorputi,* V.2:140

(18) Davlet, Maria. "Petrogliphs of ancient Enisei." The Official Journal of the Russian Academy of Science 2 (2002): 119.

(19) Dixon, O. (2008) The Mystery of Fly Agaric. N.p.: *Veligor*, 42

(20) Sevrinovsky, V. (2013, September 9) Posledny Shaman. *Vokrug Sveta,* 87

(21) Varsegov, N. (2014, January 22) Rassledovanie gibeli gruppy Dyatlova bylo nedostovernym. *Komsomolskaya Pravda.* Retrieved from http://www.kp.ru/daily/26184/3073188/

(22) Krasheninnikov, S. (1949) Opisanie zemli Kamchatki. *Glavsevmorputi,* V.2:14

(23) Varsegov, N. (2014, January 22) Rassledovanie gibeli gruppy Dyatlova bylo nedostovernym. *Komsomolskaya Pravda.* Retrieved from http://www.kp.ru/daily/26184/3073188/

(24) Kulemzin V.M. Shamans of the Khanty. Tartu, 2004:170-174

(25) Morozov, Y. (Coroner) (2013) [Video interview] in Komsomolskaya Pravda. (Producer) Retrieved from http://www.kp.ru/daily/26311.5/3189866/

(26) Tumanov, E. (Coroner) (2014) [Video interview] in Komsomolskaya Pravda (Producer) Retrieved from http://www.kp.ru/daily/26311.5/3189866/

(27) Pushkarev, I. (2016, January 18)Oni razgrabili svyaschennoe mesto. *Znak.* Retrieved from https://www.znak.com/2016-01-18/v_dele_o_gibeli_gruppy_dyatlova_novye_svidetelstva

(28) . Serdyuk, M.(Speaker). (2013) Pereval Dyatlova: ne khodi tuda [Television series episode] In Pervy Kanal (Producer), *Pust Govorya*t. Retrieved from http://www.1tv.ru/videoarchive/61020 35:03

Printed in Great Britain
by Amazon

46821078R00126